Ugly Baby

How To Get Over Fear And Give Birth To Your Odd Idea,
Start A Business,
Or Invent Something Cool.

KIM DUKE

ISBN: 1479225665
ISBN 13: 9781479225668

Published in Canada by Plunkett Press

Distributed worldwide by The Sales Divas Inc.
www.salesdivas.com

Dedicated to all the
Ugly Baby Ideas
that need to come out
screaming!

Other books by Kim Duke:

Tickled Pink: The Secrets of Attracting Delightful Customers

Table of Contents:

INTRODUCTION:

The Ugly Baby Basics

Gotcha.

I knew the title *Ugly Baby* would catch your attention! (I didn't spend 15 years slaving in the corporate trenches of national advertising for nothing)

So you're probably thinking…

"Ugly Baby …. WHAT is this and how does it apply to creating new ideas for business? And more importantly — how does it apply to ME?"

First of all — the *Ugly Baby* concept is a simple one.

And the idea came from my customers.

How?

Each time they were thinking of leaping into a new arena, a new project or venture…a large and looming shadow would cross their face and they would start pumping out excuses about WHY they couldn't do it. (Just like a teen-ager trying to escape garbage take-out duty.)

Ever had THAT feeling?

WELCOME TO THE
UGLY BABY MOMENT!

One of the greatest obstacles standing solidly in front of you and bringing your dream/idea to life is your fear of being judged. And quite frankly – it has you paralyzed. Deep down you're scared to death YOUR IDEA will be REJECTED, you'll GO BANKRUPT or you'll be skinned alive by the critics.

It feels very similar to being the last kid picked for the baseball team.

The thought of….

- Sneers
- Jeering vs cheering
- Sighs of disappointment
- Raised eyebrows
- The word NO

… cause you to inwardly cringe.

So you keep your precious little idea wrapped up tight in a sound-proof, bomb-proof box that even the Hulk, Popeye and Oprah couldn't open.

I think you're familiar with the judges.

Let's start with your peers, customers, employees, family and friends to name a few. Of course, the biggest, scariest and harshest judge of them all – is YOU.

Did I just hear your stomach flip-flop?

What's it for you? A fear of...

- Starting a business?
- Closing or selling your business?
- Launching a new product?
- Killing an old product?
- Raising your prices?
- Marketing in new uncomfortable ways?
- Starting over?
- Inventing something?
- Attracting a different target audience?
- Reversing your business model?
- Ditching your business model completely?
- Asking for a mentor to take you to the next level?
- Being creative?

Hey- remember this.

Fear is a nasty and smelly buddy.

And it also tends to show up at the worst possible times.

Fear starts nagging at you…and whispering slithery thoughts in your ear…

You've heard it before. (Most of it in your lovely head I might add)

"I can't do it."
"I need to think about this some more."
"I don't have enough time."
"What if it fails?"
"Can I find the money?"
"This is a crazy idea"
"It'll never work."
"Who AM I to be doing this?"
"I'm not smart enough"
"I'm not good enough"
"Will my customers go for it?"
"Will it sell?"
"My family and friends will think I've lost it"
"I'll get laughed out of business"
"It's too expensive"
"I'll lose money"
"I will officially end up eating cat food for the rest of my life."

Ugly Baby moments are constantly happening to me. Why? Because whenever you dream up something new and you're ready to take it into action — or do something different — the fear of your idea turning into *"An Ugly Baby"* immediately rises to the surface. And as I believe in always doing new things — you guessed it — I'm destined to have *Ugly Baby* moments along the way.

That's OK by me.

A memorable one for me (because it was so damn scary!) was when I left my big, fat corporate job as a sales manager for Canada's oldest national television network and launched my company, The Sales Divas.

(This isn't me but I LOVE her dress!)

Why did I leave? Easy. I'd outgrown the place. I felt my "wings touching the walls" and quite frankly I hate having my feathers stuck. (In fact, every job I've ever left was because of that!)

I was feeling many of the feelings you probably have right now.

I knew there was MORE INSIDE OF ME and yet I also knew if I stayed in my current job I was going to rot. I had so much to offer and it was barely being tapped or recognized. In fact, in many ways, creativity and independent thinking were discouraged. And I certainly didn't fit into the corporate mind-meld.

The year before I quit, my body was showing me that I needed to get the hell out of there. I suffered from recurring episodes of head to toe hives that looked like someone had beaten me with a baseball bat. I was black and blue all over and had puffy feet that certainly couldn't fit into stilettos (and yet I still went to work even though I could barely walk).

It was ridiculous.

Friday was the only good day of the weekend as by Saturday I was already having heart palpitations and thinking...

"Tomorrow is Sunday and that means the next day I have to go back to work."

I was dreaming constantly of having my own business — helping women entrepreneurs. Doing business differently and creatively has always been my calling card. It made me a lot of money and gave me national recognition.

However, there was a BURNING DESIRE in me to help women entrepreneurs learn how to sell and market themselves without cold-calling their fingernails off. I certainly couldn't accomplish that goal by playing it safe in my big, fat corporate job with the fancy golden "handcuffs" to match.

And so I made a vow to myself that I would plan for a year and then I would give myself the ultimate birthday gift. I lived off of one pay check per month and stashed the rest. Pedicures, manicures and massages and anything else considered not necessary became things of the past.

I opened a bank account with a title…"The Dream".

It would have been easier to have transferred the money electronically. But I needed the physical action of looking at the bank teller and saying …

"Please put this in The Dream Account."

Of course they always asked with a smile…

"What's The Dream?"

I responded with an even bigger smile and said…

"To become an entrepreneur."

Finally, after 12 long months of frugal living, saving and planning (and very rough feet); I walked into my office 2 days after my 35ᵗʰ birthday. I was resigning from the CBC Television Network. (Canada's oldest national television broadcaster)

A couple of good girlfriends drove for 5 hours to see me the week-end before. They wanted to support and encourage me before the BIG MONDAY. (Plus – I think it was a wonderful excuse to drink champagne!)

I'll never forget what my friend Lynda said:

*"Kim, a year ago you told me to tell THIS KIM she can't chicken out.
So I'm here to give you a MESSAGE FROM YOU that this is the right thing to do."*

Monday came much faster than usual.

I walked right into my office, took a deep breath and I noticed my hand was shaky as I picked up the phone to call my boss in Vancouver. My feathers shook a little too.

My boss Pat was a fabulous guy and he asked me about the office, how my birthday was etc. I filled him in and then I took a deep breath to give him my exciting news:

ME: *"Pat – I've decided to give myself an extra special birthday gift this year."*

PAT: *"Cool –what did you do?"*

ME: *"I'm resigning from CBC Television and starting my own business."*

The phone went absolutely quiet.

Silence.
Silence.
Silence.

And then…

PAT: *"NOOOOOOOOOOOOOOOOOOOOOOOOOOOO OOOOOO Kimmmmmmmm!!!"*

We ended up having a long conversation and at the end of the call he said something I've never forgotten.

"Kim, I'm jealous of what you're doing. Go for it!"

When I hung up the phone I noticed my hands were still shaking.

When I left the building for the last time almost a month later, I screamed for joy in my car as I squealed out of the parking lot!

I had made my **daring escape**.

Fast forward 3 weeks later.

On my first day as an entrepreneur, I got out of bed at 6 am, did my usual morning routine, dressed in a suit with nylons (not sure why), and as I was applying my lipstick - I looked in the mirror and said:

*"Holy *%$!## Kim!*
What have you done??"

It wasn't one of my shinier moments.

All the fears of walking away from my fast-track, big paying corporate job, all the benefits and trappings of working for a national television network came bubbling to the surface. Expense account. Pension. Box seats. Big bonuses.

And the woman in the mirror was waiting for an answer.... and she had a look of horror on her face, similar to finding a hair in your egg salad sandwich. (In my world that's the ultimate of gross.)

I looked in the mirror at the "egg-salady", panic-stricken woman who looked something like me and said:

"You CAN do this!"

I could, I would, I did and STILL DO.

And not even on my worst day, a day when cash flow was tight and I had international supplier bills rolling in the door, or when a customer was driving me nuts, or I had doubts about what I was doing...even on those kind of days I've NEVER wished to be back at my fat corporate job with the regular pay check.

One thing I know for sure:

My feathers are NEVER stuck now!

*As you get to know why and how you need to launch your idea, I hope all these free-as-a-bird-things for you, too.

I know you're having *Ugly Baby* moments right now. Take heart. They happen to all of us on a consistent basis. You're not alone.

My major *Ugly Baby* moment happened when I wrote my first book **"Tickled Pink: The Secrets of Attracting Delightful Customers"**

Writing the book was a labor of love. Getting the guts to show it to an editor and then self-publishing was NOT.

I will never forget how I felt.

As I was typing the last page and sending the file to my super smart editor …my heart was thumping, my mouth went dry, and all resemblance of my oh- so- sophisticated martini-sipping self went right out the window.

Why?

I was worried when I showed my "new born book" to the world, a project that had cost me several thousand dollars, millions of phone calls, hundreds of hours of writing, an equal amount of coffee and twice the amount of dark chocolate – they (whoever THEY are!) would look under the cover, GASP WITH HORROR and yell at the top of their lungs…

Ugly Baby!

Or worse.

They would smile a pained, frozen, thin-lipped smile and with frantically darting eyes would say…

"Oh. That's nice."

Which in the world of human psychology means…

1. It sucks.
2. You're an idiot.
3. Crappy title.
4. It will bomb.

5. No one will buy this book.
6. You don't know what you're doing.
7. This will never work.
8. You think you can write?
9. You're going to be a poor, starving writer who is forever known in the neighborhood as the Crazy Bag Lady.

Get my drift?

When I told my *Ugly Baby* analogy in my seminars to thousands of women entrepreneurs they would always crack up with laughter. As in rolling in their chairs, heads thrown back, tears making mud-pies in their mascara kind of laughter.

Why?

Whether they had kids or not – they all knew the lump in the gut, sweaty armpit "ick" feeling most of us get when we show our new creation. (Especially in business.)

I bet even Ms. J.K Rowling had the same experience when she launched her brood of *Ugly Baby* characters in the internationally acclaimed Harry Potter series.

> "It takes a great deal of courage to stand up to your enemies, but even more to stand up to your friends."

> -J. K. Rowling

A lovely friend of mine – a dear, dear friend of mine told me she had actually stashed my first book in a closet for years and finally admitted she had only *just* started to read it!

I looked at her with a frozen grin on my face.

Trust me. **Everyone** has had the **Ugly Baby** Experience.

CHAPTER ONE:

Facing Your Freaky Resistance

Let me guess.

The possibility of having someone criticize your idea (your "baby"), not jumping at the opportunity as you thought they might or ignoring it all together is about as appealing and appetizing as a bowl of lukewarm baby food.

It feels like rejection. This, in case you haven't noticed, is an emotion most people dread.

You worry.

You worry people will say, think, or finger paint this phrase on a bathroom door somewhere:

"You're not likeable, smart, brave, creative or innovative."

No one wants someone to call their "baby" ugly. That vulnerable, **"my soft stomach is exposed to the world"** kind of vulnerable is much easier to avoid than to face head on.

However, I think you need to look at this with a twist.

> "Everything has its beauty, but not everyone sees it."
>
> -Confucius

AN *UGLY BABY* ISN'T WHAT YOU THINK IT IS

Really.

I'm going to say it because I know you're thinking it.

"There's no such thing as an ugly baby."

I even had people tell me I was going to get some HEAT because of the name of this book. They told me women wouldn't like it. That most people think there is no such thing as an *"Ugly Baby"*. Well that may be true.

Now you can tell that little Pinocchio story to yourself sister -

however, both you and I know —at some time in your life you've seen a baby who would make The Bride of Frankenstein run screaming from the building.

C'mon – I made you smile didn't I? (Because you HAVE seen one!)

It doesn't mean an **Ugly Baby** is bad.
Or hopeless.
Or lacking in potential.

Or is even "ugly" at all.

Remember — "ugly" to someone is "beauty" to another. It really doesn't matter whether or not people understand why you're so passionate about your idea. What matters most, is **YOU UNDERSTAND WHY** you're so passionate. And you also have to understand IF there's a NEED for your idea in the marketplace. (More on that later — keep reading.)

She definitely needs a pedicure — wonder if she's saving up to become an entrepreneur?

Thick Skin. Your New Friend.

And trust me — once that happens — you'll discover you'll have much **"thicker skin",** a stronger sense of hopefulness and commitment and you'll be far less emotionally attached to the opinions of the "madding crowd". (And why are they so pissed off anyway??)

"Think for yourself. Unplug yourself from follow-the-follower groupthink, and virtually ignore what everyone else in your industry is saying (except the ones everyone agrees are crazy). Do your own research, draw your own conclusions, set your own course, and stick to your guns. When you're just starting out, people will tell you you're wrong. After you've blown past them, they'll tell you you're crazy. A few years after that, they'll (privately) ask you to mentor them."

— Steve Pavlina*

*(no idea who he is but Steve sure knows how to give a great sound-bite)

Remember.

The *Ugly Baby* experience is the FEAR someone will *negatively judge* what you've produced or even the idea itself. That they won't BUY IN. That they will MOCK YOU. It's the FEAR of seeing something reflected in the eyes and minds of others which disappoints you. And of course, the biggest and scariest fear you have is you'll DISAPPOINT YOURSELF in some soul-sucking way.

And THAT fear alone is kicking you in the buns and blocking you from the success, happiness, weekly blowouts at the hair dresser and travel to Paris flea-markets you so richly deserve. (Yes – I confess – these are all my secret desires!)

It gets a little tiring doesn't it?

I'm sure you've had HUNDREDS of wonderful ideas and dreams, thought of many brilliant things to say, write, start, create and do but *something* held you back like an invisible pair of handcuffs and you justified to yourself it was OK.

(Really. You LIKE handcuffs.)

You've promised yourself that you'll:

- Do it someday when the timing is better
- Put it on the back burner and you'll do it sometime soon
- Do more research, analysis, money or therapy before you can begin (heavy on the therapy here)

Ummmmmm. I don't think so.

The timing is never going to be right.
Anything put on the back burner burns or dries up.
Perfection never happens.
Ducks don't line up in a row.
Tomorrow never comes.

And then from out of nowhere you see YOUR IDEA in the news, on your competitor's website, on television, all over social-media, the big screen or in the newspaper or perhaps you drive by the little store you wanted to buy (and someone else did) and you grind your teeth and bite your nails in frustration and say …

"But I thought of that
5 years ago!!"

Hate to break it to you, cupcake, but even though you may have thought of it, you didn't do anything with it.

Just remember how the women of the world felt when Heinz — a 100 year old company, finally introduced the upside down ketchup bottle with a flat bottom.

Weren't they "speedy" with this idea?

This new "invention", created after 60 years of the damn ketchup bottle falling out of fridges all over North America, because women were balancing it on its head to get "every last drop." (You know what I'm talking about — don't deny it!)

Do you know how many kids were grounded because of the damage they did trying to get ketchup out of the bottle? Damaged curtains, their mother's white sweater, a dent in the table (OK — yes — I've just confessed my dark past with the ketchup bottle.)

Or how about the squeezable mayonnaise bottle — after 40 years of millions of women getting their hands and arms all gooey as they scraped the jar with a spatula to make a last batch of potato salad? (Been there and done that too!)

My mother had something to say about all of this...

"Kim — I've been saying they should invent these things for 40 years!"

Contrary to popular belief - all those fabulous ideas we ignore don't wither and die.

Oh no, sister.

Instead they get sucked back up into the Universal Bakery. Ever been there? It's a quaint and sparkly little place with red checkered tables and gremlins in the back working non-stop on the manufacturing of perfect ideas.

It's right on the corner of You Blew It Avenue and Na-Na-Na-Na-Na Street.

And then SOMEONE ELSE will whip up some new weird and wonderful Baked Alaska with all the luscious and simple ingredients you rejected and THEY will win the Betty Crocker prize.

And you won't even get to lick the spoon.

CHAPTER TWO:

The Bad Habit Of Being Stuck

I know you think you work hard.
I know you think you invest in yourself and your business growth.
I know you think you've got a great product or service.
I know you think you offer amazing customer service.
I know secretly you take pride in telling everyone how busy you are.

Here's a news flash for you.

It's not enough.

Your fear of not taking a chance, a risk, leaping and stretching into the unknown void doesn't just apply to how you won't try sushi, skating or skydiving in your personal life.

Nope.

It applies to your business and sales too. And it's keeping you very, very, very stuck. (Have you ever noticed what's stuck - eventually starts to smell too?)

That's what happens when you're stagnant.

As a child I spent many wonderful hours on my grandparents' farm. There was a little pond which always had a coating of green scum on it and it smelled horrific. (Truly — the smell alone made me gag).

I remember asking my grandpa what THAT was and why it smelled so bad.

His reply?

"This pond doesn't have any movement or new oxygen going into it.
It is basically water that's ROTTING."

My response then was the same as it would be today:

Yuck!

Remember lady, maintaining the status quo is a status and smelly NO!

The strange thing is HOW you become stagnant. It's not a FAST thing. It creeps in slowly, leaving a slimy trail you don't see at first.

Years ago I was teaching a seminar (about growth) and a woman threw her hands in the air and said...

"Enough already! I'm tired. When can I stop growing?"

If someone had a picture of me at that moment it would be one of me with my mouth hanging open. Maybe even some drool.

In the medical world this is called shock.

I couldn't believe what I had just heard!

My first impulse was to call a funeral home and tell them to come over here and bring a body bag and a hearse. I had one of the living dead on my hands.

However, as much as I wanted to give a smart-assed response, deep down I knew she was afraid and tired…. which in the end was creating consequences that were overwhelming and exhausting her…which was making her even MORE afraid and tired.

(Ever been there? I know I've dabbled in this bat and guano infested cave from time to time!)

And I wanted her to snap out of it.

Years ago I was visiting San Francisco and my boyfriend and I went for a hike in the Muir Woods.

If you haven't been there, put it on your bucket list. It is a magnificent, wondrous and ethereal place, with redwood trees as old and wise as time. (I felt like I'd stepped into a magical forest or at least into a Lord of the Rings movie. I kept looking for my secret crush Viggo Mortensen aka Aragorn but no luck). For a girl who loves all trees (they are incredibly special to me in more ways than one) I felt like I'd landed in a fairy tale.

The place is unbelievably beautiful and serene. The park includes redwoods over 260 feet high; some are more than 1,200 years old. Of special interest is Cathedral Grove, where delegates who drafted the charter of the United Nations held a commemorative ceremony on May 19, 1945, in tribute to President Franklin D. Roosevelt, who died in April of that year. ** Source: MSN Travel.com*

It was a first. But then so was the United Nations which was created after the devastation of WWII. They both had the opportunity to be **Ugly Babies.** And why did the first assembly of the United Nations take place right there in the woods?

Because President Roosevelt said what all nations and cultures have in common is the love of nature. It unites us.

These are incredibly ancient and massive trees (truly — they are living vegetation dinosaurs).

No matter how old a tree is, be it a redwood in the Muir Woods or a lilac bush in your backyard, it doesn't stop growing. Each year it puts down new roots and spreads its seeds to the wind and earth.

There's an old redwood tree there which was cut down in the '40s (believe me — they don't do that anymore) and it shows the timeline — all 1,200+ years of it — before Vietnam, before the 1900s, before Columbus, before Jesus…

it's a humbling experience to put your finger on the ring that represents the first year of life this tree had.

Think about it.

A 1,200 year old tree is always breaking new ground. It is always in a continual state of growth.

Guess what?

You're a tree too. And so was the woman in my seminar. Even though you may feel like you can count 1,200 wrinkle-rings on your face sometimes – you're not 1,200 years old, lady.

Instead of seeing your business or your sales as a chair that can stay the same from year to year – view it as a LIVING THING instead.

Why?

If you don't continue to grow and evolve into something better – the weeds and other stronger and more aggressive trees will CHOKE YOU OUT.

And they won't feel one bit of guilt about it either.

So there.

Are You Deluding Yourself?

It feels great to buy a book, attend conferences, online classes and live seminars, mastermind with your friends, brainstorm in the bathtub, listen to audio books and make macaroni collages of your goals.

But as my dear friend Shakespeare would say...

"Here's the rub."

Unless you read the book, take action on your best bathtub plans, listen to the audio book and apply what you've learned at a seminar or conference — you're living in the land of delusion.

Delusion.

Delusion means you're living in your head with the Tooth Fairy, Santa and the Easter Bunny.

Is it getting crowded in there, honey?

TRY: THE FLASHING SIGN SAYING YOU'RE STUCK

So often I'll hear women say "Maybe I'll try it."

Wow.

Doesn't the word TRY impress you with its clarity and confidence??

When I was a kid I would use the word TRY with my parents. "I'll try to do math, I'll try to learn <u>fill in the blank</u>." It has already started in grade school, you're afraid of committing because you might SCREW UP.

My dad always had one response:

You either DO or you DON'T.

When you DO something – sometimes it works and sometimes it doesn't. But you still DID IT. You didn't "try it" – YOU DID IT.

So if you want your idea to see the light of day – then you're going to have to go for it.

People who talk about the land of "Trying" are actually creating a safety net for themselves. They didn't commit to DOING or NOT DOING. They are in the murky gray zone called TRYING and trust me – it isn't a fun place to be. It is sort of a washed out place that makes you look like you've either had the flu for 2 weeks or at the very least – too many martinis.

So STOP using that word.

It just means you want to sit on the fence and NOT make a decision. It's an excuse wrapped up in a ratty bow.

Remember.
The only thing you get from sitting
on the fence is a **sore ass.**

If you're frustrated with how your business or your IDEA is going – sit down (preferably with a piece of chocolate) and read one of my favorite poems:

THE ROAD NOT TAKEN
– ROBERT FROST

Two roads diverged in a yellow wood,
And sorry I could not travel both
And be one traveler, long I stood
And looked down one as far as I could
To where it bent in the undergrowth;
Then took the other, as just as fair,
And having perhaps the better claim,
Because it was grassy and wanted wear;
Though as for that the passing there
Had worn them really about the same,
And both that morning equally lay
In leaves no step had trodden black.
Oh, I kept the first for another day!
Yet knowing how way leads on to way,
I doubted if I should ever come back.
I shall be telling this with a sigh
Somewhere ages and ages hence:
Two roads diverged in a wood, and I-
I took the one less traveled by,
And that has made all the difference.

Now ask yourself:

"Am I at a fork in the road and thinking of choosing the easy path?"

Or worse. (You just keep looking at the fork!)

Did you say Yes?

Then it's probably time for what I lovingly call an *Ugly Baby* **Moment.**

FACING THE *UGLY BABY* MOMENT

In my many years of selling for Canada's national television networks I had to show the world the *"Ugly Baby"* on a constant basis. Promotions, contests, new television shows were run past advertisers continually.

Some were hits with my clients. Many were flops. But the hits still out-weighed the flops. (And yes – I had to deal with rejection from my customers too!)

The most important thing to realize is if you're too afraid to show your "baby" to the world, and you let it stagnate and die – that in itself is a far bigger failure.

You'll never be embarrassed by taking a chance and giving life to your idea. It may turn out differently than you first imagined…but you're LIVING.

Now as an entrepreneur – I launch several *Ugly Baby* projects every year. It may not look like an *Ugly Baby* to you but every new project/article/video/speech/idea has to get flown by its potential customers sooner or later.

If they like it – your Ugly Baby suddenly got cuter.

If they don't like it to the degree you need them too – then your *Ugly Baby* goes back to the drawing board, you pout for awhile and then move forward.

So you see – you're not the only one worried about rejection. And it won't kill you either.

I've had TONS of *Ugly Baby* moments over the years!

One of my WORST moments was a presentation I made years ago early in my speaking career.

Why was it an *Ugly Baby*?

It was something BRAND NEW for me – doing a keynote speech in front of a large audience. The idea for the keynote was brilliant. At least *I thought so,* and I wanted to try it out in front of a large crowd.

What ended up happening?

I'm wincing as I write this…300 secretaries (who really don't like salespeople by the way), a Friday afternoon on a beautiful summer day, a gig with my business partner that was rapidly going downhill, a 2 1/2 hour presentation that should only have been 45 minutes – new material, bad speech, bad timing, bad preparation, bad chemistry, wrong message, wrong audience.

Did I also mention I danced with a broom at one point? Wearing a cheap tiara? And a feather boa? It was sad – really sad.

If the poor audience had tomatoes on their tables they would have thrown them at us for sure. Instead they filled out 300 evaluations that basically said:

"They sucked."

What I originally thought was a fabulous idea quickly became as smelly as an old cloth diaper.

I cried for 2 days. Trust me – it wasn't pretty. (I dare YOU to read 300 evaluations that basically say you have no right to exist on the planet.)

Then I decided I couldn't be a cry baby just because I had a HUGE *Ugly Baby* moment. (To be honest – it was 150 long tortuous moments actually – for both me and the crowd!)

I knew I still had a good idea but I obviously needed to get it to crawl before I made it run the 100 meter dash.

Plus, I deeply believe in this lovely Japanese proverb about success:

"Fall down seven times. Get up eight."

And then I remembered years ago being in a really cool coffee shop and bookstore called B. Macabees. (They were WAY AHEAD of their time!)

Taped to the counter beside the old fashioned cash register were tons of funny pictures, cartoons and quotes about life. One that burned into my mind forever was:

> "When you're standing at the edge of a cliff, the definition of success is moving 2 steps back."
>
> - Anon.

So I had a big girl conversation with myself.

"OK Kim —it's your choice. Are you going to feel sorry for yourself and QUIT or are you going to get back on the horse and this time take riding lessons?"

I met with the person who hired me, a fabulous, wise, gracious and kind woman I'll never forget. She looked me in the eye and said...

"Right message. Wrong crowd. But don't give up. Keep practicing."

I contacted a big name speaker I admired and asked him to mentor me. He accepted. I asked him to lunch so I could share the *Ugly Baby* Horror Story with him and get some much needed advice.

Neither of us ended up eating much – for two very different reasons.

As I was telling him my story – he kept squinting at me and laughing. (To his credit – he did try to contain himself but to no avail)

At times it was almost ridiculous.

Here I was, doing the delicate, "I- know- I -screwed -up, slow- tears out -of the- big –eyes- routine" and he was grimacing, contorting his face and basically trying not to explode with laughter and spray me with his damn salad.

Of course I couldn't eat as I was wound up like a top – trying to not CRY in front of this man I admire so much.

He laughed so hard he cried when I told him about all the details of "The Bomb" aka my Ugly Baby Moment. (Honestly, he had tears of laughter rolling into his Cobb salad. It wasn't pretty.)

When he finally quit howling with laughter -he too said something I'll never forget.

"Kim, be grateful. It could have been 300 CEOs. And you've learned a University Degree worth of business in an afternoon."

And then he said something that's burned into my DNA…

" And most importantly Kim, be grateful you weren't MEDIOCRE ENOUGH. Otherwise, it wouldn't have forced you to become better."

And it DID make me become better.

It forced me to make a decision about becoming better.

I got out of the business partnership, joined professional speaking associations, and bought every program and book on speaking I could find, gave loads of free speeches for practice, found a mastermind group and hired a top level internet marketing coach.

Most importantly? I applied IT ALL.

And it paid off.

Now I speak internationally to audiences of thousands, I'm an author of 2 books and hundreds of articles, I'm featured on international media, I'm a national magazine columnist, I have subscribers from all over the world and I have tons of fabulous clients and a lifestyle of freedom AND I can make more money in a week-end than I used to make all year. (Yes – I said that all in ONE BREATH.)

But it didn't start there. It started with a choice to NOT BE MEDIOCRE.

So now I'm saying the SAME THING to you.

I imagine you're reading this book because you want to be better....much, much, much better than you currently are. (I also think you're a little sick of feeling mediocre and stuck)

You're feeling a GAP – dissatisfaction – or let's be honest here – a hole in your soul that feels like every bit of YOU is dropping into the
BLACK PIT OF BOREDOM
DESPAIR
and SADNESS
because you know you have it in you to DO MORE with a DIFFERENCE. (Stephen Hawking can't even BEGIN to write about a BLACK HOLE this deep!)

Well that may be true; however, those zesty ideas have to get out of your head (or the trunk of your car) and dragged into some kind of reality. Ideas are a dime a dozen. What separates the "little girls in business" from "women in business" is that WOMEN will take their idea all the way and turn it into measurable action.

Remember what my mentor told me years ago –

"...be grateful you weren't mediocre enough. Otherwise, it wouldn't have forced you to become better."

Are you currently riding the Mediocre Express? And more importantly, are you ready to jump off?

CHAPTER THREE:

Thinking About "What If"?

I listen to dead people.

Now – before you get all "creeped out" – I'm talking about listening to the wise, wonderful and sometimes weird words of those who have lived and died before me.

They have taught me how the POWER OF THINKING leads to inspired action.

They have also helped me "dream up" many wonderful ideas over the years. Before anything comes into creation – *it must first be a thought*.

So I proudly admit I'm a thinker.

Quite often friends and family will catch me staring off into space and they say …

"There she goes – thinking again."

One of my favorite dead guys is Albert Einstein (by the way – did you know his last name is supposed to be pronounced

EIN- SCHTEIN? This is one of the pet peeves of my dear friend Phyllis, Buddhist, classical soprano-ist and with an IQ close to 180. She protects that large brain of hers with an impossibly ancient and puffy beaver pelt hat. (Just think of a fur dandelion).

Little known fact, but true.

Albert said:

"IMAGINATION IS WORTH MORE THAN KNOWLEDGE"

Why?

Because knowledge is based upon past experiences and imagination is based upon the future. One has boundaries and the other is limitless. Mix the 2 together and you can create sparkling opportunities that will dazzle and delight.

So often we stifle and stunt the growth of our ideas because "our knowledge" gets in the way and our imagination is jammed into the closet next to the old Christmas decorations we've been meaning to throw out.

We become a "know-it-all" which allows us to "logically" NOT take action. Einstein knew what he was talking about here. He knew when you allow your imagination to run wild (something we all have been advised against at one point or another) it will provide a force far more powerful than someone trying to connect all the dots.

Another dear and dead imaginary friend, Thomas Edison said was,

"Thinking is highly under-rated"

Think about that for a moment.

"THINKING IS HIGHLY UNDER-RATED."

We've all been taught we need to be running at the speed of light in order to be a success. This is a North American phenomenon, equating "busy-ness" with happiness.

It's probably why I'm so attracted to France. They have 35 hour work weeks, long lunches, focus on entertaining with family and friends, reading, culture and drinking wine.

No one ever said...

"Quit working and get under a tree and daydream for an hour!"

Now don't panic, this isn't a time management book, however, I think its bloody ridiculous (there's a Canadian term for you!) how we expect to grow in business and in life and yet hardly spend any guilt free time just...

Thinking.

NOT:

- doing the laundry
- walking the dog
- hitting the grocery store
- making dinner
- driving kids here, there and everywhere
- talking to employees
- satisfying customers
- buying a birthday gift for your mother
- getting the oil changed
- coffee with friends

- cleaning up
- …the list is endless.

Yes – all those things are important (or NOT!) but something just as critical to your creativity and success is good old thinking time.

I can hear it already.

"Kim – I don't have time to think or be creative– I'm too busy!"

Um. Here's my comment on this excuse.

YOU'RE IN A RUT AND IT'S MAK-ING YOU SMELL BAD!

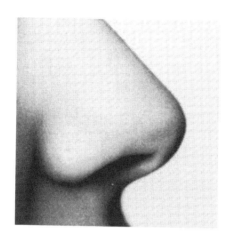

Because true living, great ideas and true success — comes most easily, quickly and creatively to people who take time to think. They make the choice.

Why? Because this is where vision and ideas come from — and they can't come from a dried up prune. (Yes — I'm talking about you!)

Everyone has 15-20 minutes a day to sit and think. And if you don't — then create it. If you want to really accelerate your business growth and ideas to the heights deep down you know you're capable of …. then pull up a chair and a cup of tea and don't fall asleep!

MOVING INTO THE WORLD OF "WHAT IF"

"I think, at a child's birth, if a mother could ask a fairy godmother to endow it with the most useful gift, that gift would be curiosity."

- Eleanor Roosevelt

Someone once told me one of my greatest traits was my **insatiable curiosity.** I thought it was one of the best compliments of my life!

Why?

If you're curious — you're not dull. In fact, you're the opposite of dull. You're razor-sharp.

You're someone who is intelligent and full of wonderment and you don't accept things at face value.

You may get into a lot of trouble.

So what.

Curiosity is definitely a trait I admire in others. Curious people tend to not be jaded and cynical — in fact they're the opposite. They are OPEN.

An idea comes to you when you're curious. A thought starts knocking about in your head as you're wondering about the status quo of something. And you begin to ask yourself the question ...

"Hmmm….what if…."

You can also *groom* curiosity.

I have a thick black book in my library and it always provokes unusual and insightful conversations. I use it when I want to imagine a new product or service and I feel I'm spinning tops in my mind.

The book is called "The Big Book of If" by Evelyn McFarlane and James Saywell and my niece is especially in love with it. In fact – she has been in love with it for years! I would pick up her and her sister and we'd go to Starbucks (hot chocolate for them – Tazo Chai Latte for me!) and I read the questions to them.

And their responses have always blown me away. Because really – who knew children think about what they would do if they ran the world?

Why would a little girl with huge brown eyes be so intrigued by The Book of IF?

Because she loves the weird questions …

- If you could rid the earth of one thing what would it be?
- If you could determine the age at which you will die, but with no guarantees regarding health or money, how old would you like to be when you go?
- If you could teach your pet to do one thing, what would it be?

- If you were allowed to eat only one vegetable for the rest of your life, which one would it be?
- If you had the gift of magic for one day, what would you do?

And even more so – she loves the responses she gets when she reads the questions to people!

I'm a big What-Iffer from waaaaaaaaaaaay back.

I'm not sure where I received the "What If "DNA but I'm blessed with it. And you may not know it but you're blessed with it too.

You just have to start asking yourself some "What If" questions to stir you up and get the creaking gray matter called your brain back to life!

In my closet – I have a sticker pasted to the top of my mirror.

It says:

"What would you do today IF you knew you could not fail?

It reminds me to "live in the zone of imagination" just as my dear, dead friend Albert Einstein suggested.

So let me ask you.

What would you do today IF YOU KNEW YOU COULD NOT FAIL?

10 "WHAT IF" QUESTIONS TO GET YOU STARTED:

1. What if my idea brings me the most happiness and joy of my life?

2. What would I do if I knew that potentially thousands of people would support my idea?

3. What if the negative things I'm saying in my mind AREN'T TRUE?

4. What if the money easily finds its way to me?

5. What if it's easier than I think?

6. What if I decided I would do ONE ACTION today to move my idea forward?

7. What if I never get this chance again?

8. What if this idea led to an EVEN BETTER IDEA but I wouldn't know unless I jumped in?

9. What if the media covered my idea because it was so unusual?

10. What if I woke up proud of myself every day for the rest of my life?

TO GET CREATIVE YOU NEED TO SURROUND YOURSELF

I know — I know. One minute I'm telling you to go under a tree and think and then the next I'm telling you to surround yourself.

Trust me — I'm not asking you to have multiple personalities. I think you have a pretty firm grip on that already.

But here's the deal. You need both.

My friend Collin, is a screenwriter in Los Angeles. We've been friends for almost 20 years and his nasty nickname for me is "Motivational Freak" as he thinks something is seriously wrong with my brain.

He may be right but all I know is these things really HELP:

- Positive people (even the ones who call you "freak")
- A creative environment
- Time to be alone
- New sources of inspiration
- Books, audio CDs, documentaries
- People that challenge and dare you to be better
- Inspiring images and reminders
- Quotes that perk you up
- Music that uplifts you
- Whatever works best for you

After my speaking engagements I often get asked…

"Kim, how do you stay so full of fun, energy and ideas?"

If they saw my home, my car, and the people in my life — they would know exactly what I do in one glance.

What do I surround myself with?

Books, mentors (living and dead), messages on my walls, amazing people, framed artwork that has positive symbolism for me, no television, magazines, beautiful things, poetry, music 4 hours per day, a tree house to write in, a 4-day work week, an office with wall-to-wall leopard carpet, chandeliers, mirrors (anything to reflect light), glittery, old glamorous objects that have a story, pictures of the people I love, a huge oil painting of my grandmother in a vintage bathing suit, bird feeders outside my windows, tons of journals and pens to capture ideas when they hit me, educational audio CDs in my car, fabulous shoes, plus a gorgeous little black dog who thinks she's human. Even my hairstylist is a Polish woman who survived poverty and Communism — she has the heart of a poet and plays classical piano and viola. And yes — also add in a healthy supply of honey mead. (Blame my Polish hairstylist — she's the one who got me hooked on it.)

Now — don't get me wrong. I'm not Polly Anna. Do I still experience bitchy, Chicken Little moments of doom and gloom — which make me resistant to sharing my ideas with the world?

Damn right.

But I probably bounce back quicker than most, simply because of how I surround my mind.

Try it. You'll like it. You may even become a freak too.

CHAPTER FOUR:

Her On-Line Paper Dolls Attracted Oprah!

OK – I can admit it. I'm an Oprah addict. Her OWN channel is incredible but the monthly magazine is how I really get my Oprah fix.

And I devour every page which led me to discover *Design Her Gals*. So what was the amazing product featured on the O List?

On-line paper dolls you create in your own image, (or choose a body type that's 10 pounds skinnier!) and you choose fashion and hair styles for FREE and then, if you so choose, you can create any number of printed products with your image on it. Or you can just send an e-card for free with your new, funky self on it.

I was hooked instantly.

I told my friends, sent out some address stickers to my clients as gifts (with their image of course) and everyone raved about how unusual it was and even more importantly – HOW FUN IT WAS.

This website was so brilliant, the product so innovative, that I contacted the founder and CEO of Design Her Gals, Jeanne Fitzmaurice, to ask her how she launched her *Ugly Baby* (as I knew something this innovative had met with resistance somewhere along the line)

This woman is a dynamo.

Jeanne for example has been interviewed nationally on the Today Show, profiled in the New York Times, was chosen as Fast Company's Fast 50 and she also is a crusader in the battle against breast cancer by donating 5% of her sales to Stage IV breast cancer research.

She's a lady you **definitely** want in your corner.

UGLY BABY INTERVIEW:

Jeanne Fitzmaurice
Founder and CEO of *Design Her Gals*

Kim:	**What inspired the idea behind Design Her Gals?**
Jeanne:	I think like many things Designer Gals happened organically and it's not unusual for the brand itself to have been built up organically as well. The idea actually came from a customer in Southern California who came to us where we had a stationary store there who wanted a personalized fairy princess birthday party invitation for a fairy princess and she couldn't find one that looked like her fairy princess. So she came to us and asked if we would design a party invitation that would look like her daughter and we did.

Jeanne: After we did that and it went out to the fairy princess's 50 best fairy princess friends and they all wanted it to look like them. They all wanted it to be a roller skater, a cheerleader or something else but they wanted it to be theirs. So from that ...the fairy princesses' mom's wanted cards that looked like them for 30th birthday parties and play date cards and things like that. So that's really where it all started.

Kim: Hopefully did the lady ever sign up for shares in the company?!

Jeanne: I don't know. I get asked all the time and one day I'm sure I'll be hearing from her! The actual idea online came much later on. We developed the line organically and sold it to stationary stores around the country in an album format where you would go and manually select your hair color, eye color, skin tone and outfits and it was a pretty laborious way to create stationary like you can today.

It was much later on after I had moved to central Oregon from Southern California with my son and husband and had probably enough fresh air and time on my hands and got to think about the brand and how I would be able to connect and reach out to a broader range of women that we actually took it online.

Jeanne: We launched it online in September of 2005.

Kim: **It wasn't much longer after that that I read about you in O magazine. That's exactly how I found out about your company and quickly became a customer.**

Jeanne: Yes that's an excellent point and you had asked me something about what we did that was a little bit different in our marketing strategy. I would say we put value on and trusted the value on what I call the underground, the viral nature of world today. And that viral nature can make or break you. So we had a pretty clear idea of what the passion and purpose of our brand was going to be, we were committed to the authenticity of that and trusted in those who would help to want to make that a success for us. And it proved to be true.

Just to add a piece to the story, the day I decided to develop the brand on line and to create it into their inter-activity product ...no sooner than I had made that decision I got a phone call from one of my very best friends who told me her best friend (who we had just walked the breast cancer 3 day walk with 2 months prior) had been diagnosed with stage 4 breast cancer, which is incurable. I knew there was something very serendipitous about that phone call. I had an epiphany that day. I will never forget that moment or day for the rest of my life and realized my decision to take these gals online had a much great purpose then what I had thought about at the moment I had made the decision.

That was to bring awareness to a piece of the breast cancer disease that people didn't necessarily want to talk about and do it in a fun and whimsical way.

Kim: **Absolutely and you're donating 5% of your sales with your foundation, which I think is absolutely fantastic.**

Jeanne: In my opinion you can't afford to not have a pay it forward component to your business model. I think that that's what keeps businesses alive, that's what keeps your customer base supporting you and that's what really does generate the desire in others to want to help support your business and help it grow.

Kim: **And women are natural pay it forward kind of people. What are some of the biggest challenges you faced before you launched this? Was it the technology component? Were you thinking where the heck do we even begin with creating all of this?**

Jeanne: Certainly developing an interactive website without any web development experience whatsoever was a huge challenge. I'm not afraid to say I'm over 50 years old and the web as I knew it when I went to college, the hard drives filled complete rooms. Growing up, a net was something you used to catch butterflies in. So definitely the internet as we know it today did not exist.

So finding the right strategic partners to work with who understood my goals and objectives was a must and I definitely recognized that was going to be very key and integral to the success of the business. It was the platform to which I was going to get the brand out there to the large community base that we now serve.

I didn't understand ANY element whatsoever of web development- it was my biggest challenge.

Kim: **But you can hire people to help you with that component. It's all about** having the vision of what you want to see. Its just like I don't need to know how my car engine operates, I just need it to get me to the hair stylist.

Jeanne: Right but you need to know that you have a good mechanic to make sure that it's going to operate when you need it too!

Kim: The concept of this whole book is about women overcoming and stepping beyond the fear of either being ridiculed by even family, friends, and co-workers where people say "Oh God that's just such a stupid idea. Don't even go ahead with it." And it holds so many good people and so many good ideas back.

Did anybody tell you "Jeanne, this is crazy?"

Jeanne: I guess I've always listened to my inner self and seek out those who are going to support me. Not to say they're going to say that everything I'm doing is great and swell but to find and focus on those who are going to support your idea in a positive and constructive way.

Kim: Women are out there and going "okay I'm going to go for it" and they've got the courage, they scrounged up the money and then something happens they're not expecting. They didn't get the positive response they were looking for or it wasn't overwhelmingly positive. You know how that happens, everybody starts a database and they think millions of people are going to come and find me right away. Well, it sometimes takes a bit of work to get that happening. I know I certainly felt that.

Kim: What would you recommend to women if they don't get the response they're looking for right away?

Jeanne: I guess the first thing that comes to mind for me is drill deeper. Try to understand what responses you were hoping for and compare it to the responses you got and ask yourself some questions like "was this less or more?" Plan for the best and prepare for the worst. I think you always have to have a Plan B and C and D and you need to be flexible.

Flexibility in launching businesses is so important because it never will look exactly as you thought. The one thing you can plan on when you make a plan is it won't be the way you planned it.

Kim: **Exactly. Most of the cases for me it's usually worked out for the best even though at the beginning I bitched about it.**

Jeanne: Quite frankly its really important if you want to be an entrepreneur or launch a business to be flexible because if you're going to be set and things don't work out the way you expected and you're no open to other options, you probably won't succeed at it.

Jeanne:	Drill a little bit deeper, try to understand what the responses have been. Are they just different or is there something significant to why they didn't go the way you had hoped? Is there something you can gain from the information? In most cases or in many cases your results aren't keeping sync with your market projections and many women don't even have those, so they wouldn't even know. Just as in Seth Godin's book, The Dip, you need to decide whether you're in a dip or on a cul-de-sac and that means knowing whether or not this is a matter of deciding who is going to be the fairest of them all and you need to keep at it a bit longer and tighten your girth or you need to move on. Failing fast there is nothing wrong with failing fast.
Jeanne:	I think so many of us hold onto those sacred cows and those are beliefs we have. The best thing in the world we're bringing to the universe and everybody is going to embrace it in seconds. It's just like the websites, if you build it

they will come. That is so far from the truth.

Kim: **Exactly, the Field of Dreams.**

Jeanne: If you build it it's built. Then you're just like a store or anything else you have to get your word out there, you have to let people know you're there. From that perspective you asked about the non-traditional kind of approaches but trusting in the organic nature of the brand and the ability for those such as yourselves out there to help us build our success, I also had very little money to dedicate to marketing and I chose to dedicate it all to publicity.

Kim: **Oh you're a smart girl!**

Jeanne: From there I committed the balance of my money to supporting the site and the community I was to serve and being responsive and recognizing the internet was very high tech and our brand was very high touch. So we have really truly committed technology to

be able to address and respond and react to our community in a pretty high
touch way and that allows us and myself to speak to over 200 different individuals daily.

Jeanne: One of my mentors and one of the individuals on my board of advisors and
I highly recommend any entrepreneur
out there to surround themselves with a
good board of advisors. And those are
individuals who are going to help get
them to where they're trying to go and
are good people to access as resources.
On my board of advisors is a woman
whose name is Mary Lou Quinlan. She
has written a book called *Just Ask a Woman*.

She and her company were very in-
strumental in helping me launch my
brand. Again, I'm sort of bouncing
around but another piece of advice I'd
give anyone out there who is thinking
about launching a business is don't be
afraid to ask others to help you, even
those who seem out of your range,
out of your realm. You knew you

would be surprised how many individuals, women in particular just like you said are willing to help support what you're trying to do.

I get hundreds of emails a month from women trying to launch businesses who ask for my thoughts. I dedicate myself to giving back to those who are asking because lots of people have been there for me too.

Kim: I feel exactly the same way. I always tell people I didn't get here on my own stilettos. I was always on the shoulders of others as well, people who were willing to help me get to the next level. It's about reciprocity. I absolutely believe that.

So last but not least what was the biggest surprise out of everything that you just never expected would happen when you launched the business?

Jeanne: Well that's a great question. I dreamed so big I don't know if I had the biggest surprise.

Jeanne: I guess the natural answer would be when I got chosen by Oprah for her list. That would seem like it should have been the biggest surprise. Surprised isn't the word, I was so grateful how well received our brand has been to so many women around the world. If there was any surprise, it would have to be how many women have now become my friends and I have had the wonderful opportunity to connect with even albeit virtually through the internet. I'm amazed at the power of the internet. I guess that would probably be my biggest surprise.

Kim: **I just love it. I think it's such a brilliant way of developing relationships with people that you never would have met.**

Kim: **It's like the world's biggest love letter, one of those chain letters you send out to people.**

Jeanne: It definitely a party in a box. Not only that but an incredible network of resources and ability to learn and grow

> and develop your product and certainly Google may be the most powerful search engine giant, I think it's the Woogles out there, the women who are online generating giggles and love everywhere!

Jeanne Fitzmaurice created an on-line business that came from having an Ugly Baby Idea and then being willing to launch it to the world.

Design Her Gals made almost 2 million dollars in its first year (Who said that 35-55 year old women don't want to make on-line paper dolls??)

And P.S.

As of this printing — Jeanne has been so successful with her site that she's now sold it and moved on to other new exciting opportunities. A true entrepreneur!

CHAPTER FIVE:

All or Nothing Is For Sissies

A phrase that drives me absolutely crazy is when people say *"It's ALL or Nothing for me."* Or here's another "favorite": *"Go Big or Go Home."*

Oh please.

It's SO cave man.

"Me drag meat to cave or me DIE."

Except you're not a cave man. And if you're reading this book my bet would be you're probably not a man. I don't think you have to drag meat anywhere – a chocolate bar MAYBE but not meat.

Why do you need to kill this Neanderthal thinking?

It's too **big**.

And when something is too big, most people choose to stay away from it and ponder their dilemma from a safe distance for…I don't know….a decade or two.

The problem? (I know YOU know the answer to my question!)

Fabulous ideas, fresh beginnings, exciting dreams, new ways of doing things, creativity, art, inventions, friendships, connections and discoveries never see the light of day.

Think about that for a moment. Look around you. Do a little twirl! For every single item and service you use in your home and business, right down to the little aspirin you take for a head-ache…first began as an idea in someone's mind. Everything you see was the result of an entrepreneur.

And now look around you again. Because for every fabulous "idea" that now surrounds you and makes your life (or someone else's life) better in a thousand, inexplicable little ways….also realize millions of ideas that were even *better* were *never brought to life*.

The main reason was because of these ridiculous "All or nothing" and "Go big or go home" beliefs.

Now don't think this is a contradiction from what Jeanne Fitzmaurice said about "Fail Faster. "She knows the sooner you can launch your idea and fine-tune it — the better off you are!

But so many people feel they have to create it PER-FECTLY first so they can launch it in a BIG WAY.

And then they never do.

A cure for cancer by taking a vitamin, a vehicle that uses garbage as fuel, the perfect pair of jeans you need to only try on once and it magically conforms to your body and melts 10 pounds of lard...who knows of all the miracles that would and could be invented if people were willing to courageously face their **Ugly Baby** moment! (And if you're the person inventing the jeans that magically take 10 pounds off my behind—please email me...asap!)

ARE YOU TRAPPED IN "SOMEDAY QUICK SAND?"

There have been so many people over the years who have told me they want to write a book. In fact, it is one of the main goals most people will say and yet NEVER act on.

I always say "GO FOR IT! ", and then a year or two later I'll bump into them somewhere and ask about their book. And they hum and haw, look at their feet, then at the ceiling and say… "Nooooo – I haven't gotten around to it yet." Or they say…

"Oh – I'm writing it in my head first."

Well that really sucks. I was hoping to buy a copy and read it. (P.S. It's really difficult to buy a book still invisibly locked in YOUR head)

I know it's tough. They are stuck in "Someday Quick Sand" and I know it's painful for them (or for you if you're one of those people dreaming about writing a book or anything else for that matter).

Why is it painful?

Well – first of all, years spent in quick sand means only one thing.

I'd bet little gritty sand particles have crept into every part of you and it's NOT comfortable, honey! (It's not like rolling around on the beach making out with someone aka the famous kiss scene between Deborah Kerr and Burt Lancaster in the movie From Here To Eternity) Plus – you can't seem to see a way out – you feel overwhelmed, trapped and in many ways, that you don't have a right to live your idea.

It's also exhausting!   And you're not an oyster so unfortunately you're NOT making any pearls with irritating sand either.

You flail around in your own mind endlessly; believing **you're stuck without choices**. When in fact, just as with "quick sand" – you CAN get yourself out.

And it's MUCH easier than you think!

And here's the "nasty" yet….YET it seems every time *we don't move forward* on what we dream of….a part of us seems to wither and crumble.

I don't know about you but I don't like feeling like a dried up prune. (I know you don't either)

Here's a poem my delightful friend Sue sent me:

A DREAM DEFERRED
BY LANGSTON HUGHES

What happens to a dream deferred?
Does it dry up
like a raisin in the sun?
Or fester like a sore—
And then run?
Does it stink like rotten meat?
Or crust and sugar over—

like a syrupy sweet?

Maybe it just sags
like a heavy load.

Or does it explode?

Doesn't this poem capture the feeling of discontent we feel when we're NOT DOING WHAT WE SHOULD BE DOING? When we're letting our ideas dry up like some cheesy Hollywood actor who spent too many years in the sun wearing baby oil?

AN AUTHOR YOU DON'T KNOW AND WON'T FORGET

In the city close to where I live is an author most people probably haven't heard of. His name is Ernie Zelinski, www.erniezelinski.com, and at the time of printing of this book he has sold over 700,000 books internationally.

He doesn't have an agent.
He self-publishes and controls the design of his books.
He has secured both North American and foreign distribution.
He's in major media constantly across Canada and the USA.
He's done it all by himself.

I had heard of Ernie and then I stumbled upon one of his books "How To Retire Happy, Wild and Free" I loved his light-hearted but straight forward style and decided to contact him and ask him for an interview.

Remember – nothing ventured – nothing gained.

He said yes and we met in the same coffee shop where he wrote his first book.

The first thing you notice about this soft-spoken and gentle man is that he LIGHTS UP when he talks about his writing journey.

I asked him HOW he accomplished such an amazing feat — selling over 700,000 books without an agent, by self-publishing and also negotiating all of his own North American and foreign distributors FOR YEARS. (Oh — and did I forget to mention he's never taken a writing class?)

Ernie replied:

"I have a motto. Do it badly. But do it."

I may have to get that tattooed on my ass.

Ernie started his writing career as a self-published author because he wasn't happy working in a normal job.

He felt discontent. And you probably are feeling it too. But there's some delicious goodness in your misery.

"May you love your discontent as it means you are on the cusp of growth."

-Henry Thoreau

You can choose to WAIT which of course is a strategy that hasn't been working for you so well.

Or you could do as Ernie says and…

"Do it badly. But do it."

I think it's time to get a move on don't you??

GET READY TO TAKE-OFF WITH THE PILOT PROJECT!

There's a perfect remedy for over-coming the Myth of Go Big or Go Home. And don't worry – you don't have to be Einstein to make it happen.

But it will require some creativity (which I KNOW you have or you wouldn't have been drawn to this book!)

Here's the formula:

1. I want you to think big.
2. And then (don't laugh!) I want you to think small.
3. And then think big again!

First off let's dive into the world of thinking BIG.

Most people I know tend to have squashed their ideas into a little ball so tight and small it reminds me of those weird travel washcloths that look like giant vitamins. You add water and POOF the thing becomes a beach towel!

We need to add some water to your dehydrated mushroom idea and make it EXPAND into dimensions you never thought were possible.

LET YOUR MIND GO KING KONG ON YOU!

Take your dream, your idea - the smoking hot thought that keeps you awake at night and BLOW IT UP it so it feels so bizarre, so uncomfortable, and so huge you're actually squirming.

Do you want to sell some kind of product to Hollywood Stars?

Own a flower shop that only does flower arrangements which look like famous works of art?

Is it your fantasy to start your own business selling products from France?

Do you want to work from home and be an internet millionaire?

Give travel tours in Europe several times per year?

Have an artisan bread bakery that ships bread around the world?

Be the first woman to own a car dealership for women in your city?

Run a coffee shop and book store and have famous authors come give readings?

Would you like to have a GREEN business — helping other businesses to go green as well?

Oh my — this list could be endless!

The key is to THINK BIG LADY! Don't deny yourself the joy of imagining your ideas in a Super-Sized Way. (Its calorie free)

I want you to throw out every negative thing you've ever been told about your imagination, creativity, "crazy ideas", yearnings, longings and dreams, desires and passion for life.

And I do mean THROW IT OUT — as it is just garbage. (Someone else's garbage by the way.) And it probably came from people who never in a million years would have thought of an idea as brilliant as yours!

Plus — they're just jealous because YOU'RE GOING FOR IT and they're *too chicken* to live their dream.

So there.

And at this point, don't worry about the logistics, the money, or the technical details. This is just time to be crazy and to stretch your ideas into areas where no one (especially you!) has gone before.

Pretend you're a kid if it helps. My niece can go from imagining herself as a dog, a teacher, a vet, a rock star, a weight lifter and back to being a dog all within 20 minutes.

This is time to GO KING KONG. Collage it, write about it, and think so huge it makes your brain hurt. (Did I tell you I actually know someone who ATE her macaroni collage in her bedroom when she was 9 because she was sent to bed without supper?)

How Sara Crewe! (OK – if you didn't read THAT book as a child get thee to a bookstore)

Think BIG. BIG. BIG. BIG.

"Life shrinks or expands in proportion
to one's courage."

- Anais Nin

And thennnnnnnnnnnnnn...

You Move Into The Shrinking World Alice!

You'll start thinking "small" – but the SMART kind of small!

I want you to test your BIG idea in a myriad of smaller ways.

THIS IS CALLED A PILOT PROJECT.

And it's a technique used in everything from film making, science, software and mathematics and sales to launching a lemonade stand on the corner when you were a kid.

The purpose of a pilot project is simple. You're testing in a smaller manner to see if your idea will FLY. Have legs. Float the boat. You get the picture!

Here are some of the Pilot Project components:

- It reduces RISK.
- It acts as a method of "convincing." Shows proof of concept.
- It allows you to survey the marketplace.
- You can test and track the results in a controlled environment.
- It stops you from alienating future customers.
- You can fine-tune any problems quickly.
- You can evaluate to see if there's a demand for what you're offering.
- It helps to create a process that can be "rolled out" in a bigger fashion.

In my former world of national television advertising, I saw this strategy used by most national corporations (the smart ones anyway!).

One of the world's fastest growing and largest franchises is Subway. (Currently they are second only to McDonalds in terms of growth and size).

2 of the biggest secrets to their success?

1. **Baking their bread on-site** (which was started by a local franchise owner who wanted to improve his product and then the idea was adopted by the rest of the chain).

2. Another key to Subway's ongoing expansion was innovation and **taking convenience** a step further than its competitors. Subway stores began appearing in **unusual locations**, <u>catering</u> to consumers where they might not expect a sandwich shop--at convenience stores and truck stops.* *Source: (AskTheDoctor.com)*

Both of these ideas had the potential to be labeled as Ugly Babies —however — the partners of Subway rolled the dice and came up with BIG DOUGH!

Another company who is brilliant at this (even if you hate their nasty fake food as I do) is McDonalds. They don't do ANYTHING without first launching the product into specific, smaller niche markets and then they test and track the results.

Remember the McRib Sandwich? Yes — it died a rubbery death and stopped McDonalds from "Going Big or Going Home" and losing a fortune in the process.

Here's another example from the food industry (and NO, I'm not writing this with a growling stomach!)

Most restaurants will also open a NEW restaurant with a "Soft Launch". They don't open with guns blazing, major advertising, contests, huge signage etc.

They'll do a **Soft Launch,** invite family, friends, suppliers etc. to come and test out the menu and the process. They want FEEDBACK. Why do they do this? Most restaurants FAIL and they can't take the chance of serving bad food with poor service.

Most ideas when they are first launched usually need some fine-tuning.

Every prototype needs it…it's an evolution of sorts.

Even Michelangelo did it.

When Michelangelo was asked HOW he made the statue of David, he replied:

"I just kept carving away what WASN'T David."

Michelangelo believed the piece of art already was within the medium. And before he would have set his chisel to marble, defining his VERY BIG IDEA — you can bet he had sculpted several different and smaller versions out of clay and marble.

You're the same way. You're a little-ol-Ms-Renaissance-Woman.

WHAT YOU CAN LEARN FROM NEW YORK

Recently I was in New York (yes – it is possible to fall in love with a city!) visiting a good friend who lives there. Dale is a native New Yorker and knows the place like the back of her hand. She has been visiting the Metropolitan Museum of Art every Saturday for years (because of its ever changing art exhibits).

They don't call this place The Big Apple for nothing!

I think it's because New Yorkers love to eat – and they love eating out as the average NY apartment has a kitchen the size of a postage stamp. (I always loved how Sarah Jessica

Parker's character on Sex And The City used her kitchen cupboards, stove and fridge to store her expensive shoes!)

As Dale and I were walking down the sidewalk on the Upper West Side of Manhattan, I couldn't believe how many restaurants there were. And they all seemed to be STUFFED FULL of customers!

I asked Dale…

"How do all these restaurants make it here?"

She replied:

"They have to be very good.
New York won't stand for anything less.
A bad restaurant won't last a month here
as there are too many other fantastic options."

She was right! No matter where we ate in New York — whether the food was from a little bakery on the corner, Zabar's famous deli or from a gorgeous and expensive Italian restaurant — the food was mouth-watering good.

You can bet these restaurants did a soft launch as quickly as they could. Why? They knew they had to offer the right food, at the right location, at the right price, to the RIGHT crowd…and they had to iron out the kinks as soon as possible if they were to succeed!

So I want you to think of YOUR idea for a minute.

Whether it's opening a high-end flower shop, starting an internet based business, selling to an entirely new group of potential customers (that no one else in your company has thought of yet) or any other cool and interesting idea you have….think about what you could do to create a "pilot project".

FIRST.

It will make help make your idea more palatable to your boss, customers, bankers and maybe even your spouse!

Here are some random ideas…

Could you…

- Hold a garden party (just like Oprah did) and invite key women in your community? You could even align with a charity at the same time.

- Create a sample group who will test your product for a certain period of time?
- Attend an event with a GARGANTUAN amount of samples (with your contact info and a call to action of course!)
- Send out an exclusive invite and ask for their ie/ taste buds, feet, "the girls" to RSVP back? (Of course your invite is focused on helping those particular areas)
- Try out this new venture by working for someone who does the same thing in another country? Even for 2 weeks?
- Do a strategic alliance with another company — your product or service could be the "added value" for their customers as a limited time offer?
- Provide a series of Free Lunch and Learn Sessions to corporations that would be a great fit?
- Hold a contest in the media and ask people to sign up for your pilot project?
- Volunteer to work for someone who is already doing what you'd love to do?

HERE'S A BIG SALES DIVA HINT: YOU HAVE TO SELL YOUR IDEA

OK — you may hate the ideas of sales but because I'm The Sales Diva I have to share this with you!

As I mention in my book **Tickled Pink: The Secrets of Attracting Delightful Customers** - you HAVE to be willing to sell your idea. You have to know inside out, backward and forward, sideways and upside down WHY your idea is the best, why it will work, who it will work BEST for and what you hope to accomplish for the customer.

And there has to be a way for people to SAMPLE YOU (I call it hors d'ouevring!) which helps the "buying process" easier for the people you want to convince. As I mentioned earlier in the book — it doesn't matter if you have an idea simply for your personal life or if you have an idea for a business venture — you have to get your idea out there so it has a chance of living!

This is why I encourage Pilot Projects to my clients on a regular basis. I know they work.

And as you combine pilot projects with surveys and evaluation — you'll discover you don't have to be afraid your idea will be an *Ugly Baby*.

Instead it provides you with a much easier method of launching, researching and testing WHAT you want to do. Whether it is opening a Bed and Breakfast on the lake or wanting to take a year off and travel the world.

Think **BIG.**

Think small.

Then think **BIG** again.

CHAPTER SIX:

The Art of Looking Sideways

Two of my favorite books on the planet are absolute contradictions.

The first, "The Art of Looking Sideways" is one of the heaviest (it literally weighs about 10 lbs), most treasured and most unusual books I own. It was as if the British author, Alan Fletcher, couldn't stop the magical (and often twisted!) river of words, images and ideas flowing from his mind.

I love how he's described at the back of the book:

"He has tackled every facet of design with a unique style and purpose, and no one else inhabits the world of ideas, of wit and ambiguity in graphic design in quite the same way. He has come to be seen as the man who took all that less-is-more, form-follows-function dogma and somehow found a way to, well, relax."

The book is peculiar, makes you think twice, twists and stretches your mind into unbelievable shapes and quite frankly, it challenges and sometimes humbles you when you realize you've been living in a tiny, little, brain box!

And it was with great sadness I learned that he passed away. All of the mind scribblers of the world will miss him and his delightful quirky mind.

The Art of Looking Sideways is a philosophy I've absolutely absorbed into my creative DNA. When you're in the process of creating; the first thing that needs to go out the window is linear thinking. Why?

Because creativity isn't linear, Little Miss Sunshine!

And yet we're taught as children to stay within the lines, the clouds should be blue and the cows shouldn't be purple.

Oh Yeahhhhh — who said??

IN FACT, CREATIVITY LOOKS SOMETHING LIKE THIS INSTEAD:

'Creativity takes courage.'

Henri Matisse

You can probably imagine what a terror it was for my editor to work her way through my book. Chapter 15 was followed by Chapter 1, then Chapter 13....no wonder she's tempted to drink martinis at 2 pm in the afternoon! (Just teasing Sue!)

Reading books like this one and allowing yourself to float in the "weirdness pool" on a regular basis, will give you the confidence to not only create what has been scampering around in your brain….it will also give you the courage to face that people may call your idea an **Ugly Baby**.

You'll be surprised with what absorbing the lessons of creativity of others will do for you. It will help you to let the sour words of people who are dumping on your idea, to run gently off your back and into the toxic pool they belong in. I call it "Acid Rain" and it certainly doesn't belong on you.

IN fact – learning how to have the "Art of Looking Sideways" you'll be inspired, fired up, challenged by those (including ourselves sometimes) who want to hold you back.

"I invented this rule for myself. I would sort out all the arguments and see which belonged to fear and which to creativeness, and other things being equal, I would make the decision which had the larger number of creative reasons on its side."

- Katharine Butler Hathaway

One of my other favorite contrarian books, "The Dip" is one of the smallest books I own. The author Seth Godin, is an internationally renowned marketing genius that I secretly have a crush on. (His brain anyway!)

Why do I admire his stuff? Seth absolutely lives in the world of Einstein, Mae West, Madonna and Amelia Earhart to name a few.

Why?

He consistently and insistently challenges convention.

And you should be too.

In order for your baby idea (ugly or not) to have the greatest amount of success, **it must be unconventional.**

Why?

If it is just more of the same that's already out there – there won't be a demand for it. People will then only buy from you if you're cheap. Also – it means you're copying vs inventing. And those who copy also have to settle for offering their product at a much cheaper price.

And people don't look to you as a leader.

Think of Martha Stewart. Then think of all the wanna-bees who have tried to copy her.

"Imitation is always a pale version of the original." (I wish I'd come up with that line!)

So let's take a quick look at what the dictionary says about what **conventional** means anyway:

Dictionary.com Unabridged (v 1.1) -

con·ven·tion·al

—adjective

1. conforming or adhering to accepted standards, as of conduct or taste: *conventional behavior.*
2. pertaining to convention or general agreement; established by general consent or accepted usage; arbitrarily determined: *conventional symbols.*
3. ordinary rather than different or original: *conventional phraseology.*

Isn't the hair on the back of your neck standing up because of how exciting these definitions sound?

Cough.

Conventional *anything* doesn't attract customers willing to pay a mid-range to premium price.

When people want normal, they head to Walmart. As they know it will probably be there and it will be for the cheapest price.

If you want to create and produce the cheapest product for Walmart — then drop this book and take it to your nearest Goodwill Donation box. My job is over.

However, if you're someone with a product or service — or an idea that doesn't fit into the Wally-World model — hey, you bought the right book!

USING THE ART OF LOOKING SIDEWAYS ON YOUR IDEA

Petunia, I'd bet you're probably **too close** to your idea at the moment.

You're so enraptured, in love, passionate, and obsessed with HOW you think it SHOULD be —it may be tough for you to think of new perspectives.

It has certainly happened to almost every entrepreneur I know. You're practically cross-eyed from looking at the details of your business and the big picture is lost completely. You can't see the flaws.

Here's a funny mental visual for you.

It is based on my secret alter-ego. (not so-secret now!)

Bugs Bunny.

Remember the scene from Bugs Bunny where Elmer Fudd is a cannibal in the jungle and he has Bugs tied up in an HUGE cauldron over a very hot fire? Elmer is throwing in carrots, potatoes and onions and singing a tune of "wascally wabbit" joy as he dances around the steaming stew pot.

Bugs dips his finger into the hot water (the very water he's sitting in) and he says…

"Yeahhhhhhhhhhhhhhh — smack, smack — I think this needs MORE salt."

Bugs was wayyyyyyy too close to his subject matter (he WAS the stew!) and I think we often end up just like him.

Stewing in our own juice and not being open to other seasonings…or not getting out of the damn pot and boiling water!

TIP YOUR IDEA SIDEWAYS AND UPSIDE DOWN!

So let me give your idea a big 'ol Mexican piñata shake for a minute. As I was thinking and writing about Bugs Bunny, my mind immediately jumped to another Looney Tunes character:

Speedy Gonzales the mouse!

I love Speedy. He's incredibly smart and kind and he loves making the action happen.

> "Money loves speed."

> - Dan Kennedy

So let's stick with the Mexican theme and I want you to imagine the biggest piñata you've ever seen. It's a piñata BIG ENOUGH to hold your idea.

Really.

Get crazy here and imagine me swinging a stick at your idea, (in my stilettos of course) with NO BLINDFOLD as I know if I knock it about and hit a hole in the side all the goodies will fall out.

Now don't be a cry baby – this is a good exercise for you!

Does Your Idea:

- Have at least one compelling and unusual feature?
- Target a large enough buying segment?
- Have a demand in the market place?
- Have opportunities to tap into more than one market?
- Make you feel you're making a difference?
- Make your customer's life easier in some way?

- Have a great idea for the media?
- Solve a major problem?
- Is viral – makes it easy for others to share the "word"?

My sister and I used to do lots of berry picking with my mother when we were children. Saskatoon berries (definitely a Canadian addiction!), raspberries, strawberries — you name it.

And as most children do — more berries ended up IN ME vs in the bucket.

I remember my mom asking me how I was doing (as she glanced inside my near empty pail) and my 8 year old berry-stained self said:

"See? I've picked them all — there aren't any more left."

Mom said…

"KIM — don't move!"

I remember thinking a bear was headed my way so I froze.

(Note: The only bear for 100 miles was the stuffed pink teddy bear on my bed)

She said:

"I don't want you to move your feet one inch. Just turn to the side as if you were a teapot pouring tea."

This "teapot" turned to one side and then I saw it.

Hundreds and hundreds of raspberries had been RIGHT IN FRONT of me except I needed to change my perspective *to be able to see them*.

I didn't have to work any harder to get the berries. I just needed to be willing to change my viewpoint.

SO WHERE DO YOU NEED TO BE "RASPBERRIED"?

Your idea has value.

And it probably has more value than you think.

But just as the raspberry story shows – we can sometimes be so SURE we have thought of all the angles –we forget to tip our perspective into a different angle!

REMEMBER – FABULOUS IDEAS COME FROM EXPANSION AND WARP

Your idea will typically have the best success if it EXPANDS or WARPS on something already in place. A root need.

For example let's consider Jeanne Fitzmaurice's online paper doll product. She understood her target customer ALREADY KNEW what a paper doll was. She didn't have to waste time and money EXPLAINING WHAT a paper doll was — or even more importantly — WHAT an ON-LINE paper doll was. Or how much FUN they are to share with your girl-friends (whether they are 4 or 40)

Or look at SPANX.

This amazing product became a massive success within a very short period of time. Sara Blakely as a young entre-preneur challenged the old-fashioned idea of a girdle, or support pantyhose and took it to a new level. Women GOT IT — they knew the benefits of a garment that made you look 10 pounds thinner but they certainly didn't want to be slapped into some 1950's cone bra. (We'll leave that for Madonna)

And you guessed it.

There are hundreds of entrepreneurs out there right now who are taking the idea of the SPANX product and giving it their own twist. Because one of the biggest complaints about SPANX is you certainly wouldn't want anyone to see you in them!

As super model Tyra Banks recently said:

"When you put SPANX on, they look like your Granny's underwear but when your dress goes on overtop – voila – you have smooth curves!"

And I guarantee SOMEONE out there RIGHT NOW is going to create a product that not only gets rid of the lumps, bumps, muffin-top and back-fat, it will also look sexy as well. (And it won't leave those "grilled panini lines" all over your body either.)

Someone will see the problem with FRESH EYES!

LOOK AT THE ORDINARY IN A NON-ORDINARY WAY

My friend Bev lost her mother several years ago. She was recently visiting her father who wanted Bev to sort through her mother's things in the basement and take what she wanted.

As she was in the musty basement a battered shoe box in the corner of the room caught her eye.

It was a shoebox full of many different pieces of wood and stones. And on the top of the shoebox, Bev's mother had written in felt marker:

"They are beautiful if you look at them the right way."

Today Bev has the unusual rocks and pieces of wood on display in her home — and she framed the lid of the shoe-box with her mother's black felt marker handwriting. It hangs right over the display.

Why? Bev wants a constant reminder to **change her perspective.**

IT'S TIME TO STIR THE POT

I'm a big fan of Stirring The Pot.

Sure, sure — some people are all about the simmering and keeping the lid on — but typically if you don't have the time to wait forever (and who does?) then you need to create some action.

What does stirring the pot do? It accelerates the action, it blends things together, it lets you know what's needed and it stops things from burning to the bottom!

It too — acts as a means of gaining a new perspective.

7 STIR THE POT QUESTIONS:

1. Do you love your idea or are you in love with the idea of an idea?

2. Is your idea life-altering? For whom?

3. What would it feel like if your idea was the PERFECT DECISION?

4. What would you do if it wasn't the perfect decision?

5. Who is a person you can talk to who always sheds a new light for you?

6. What and who are you comparing your idea to?

7. Who could you ask for help on this?

"Good things happen to those who hustle."

-Anais Nin

So.

Are you hustling or are you hedging on getting fresh perspective?

Slap on some new glasses girl!

CHAPTER SEVEN:

Are You Calling MY Baby Ugly???

As I first mentioned in Chapter 1 – one of the toughest things in life to deal with is rejection. It can feel like someone is force-feeding you cod-liver oil.

Take heart o' brave one.

I would much rather hang out with the individual who has courage and guts to play the game vs the couch potato fan on the sidelines. Terminal observers don't get far in life unless they are in astronomy, bird watching or playing a forensic scientist on TV.

As my petite 5'2 friend Jo says:

"You've got to put some skin in the game."

This is from a woman with a poverty-stricken childhood, who lost her father at a young age, who raised 2 kids on her own, survived cancer, lost a kidney, began running, learned how to drive in her 30's, taught herself how to swim at 35 so she could be in a triathlon, and who has run

23 marathons. And that's just the softer side of her life! (She's definitely put skin into the game!)

When I first decided to become a speaker on the subject of sales, I can honestly say, something I didn't think about ahead of time was being REJECTED.

Thank God for that. If I had known what I know now – I may have made a different decision!

As a speaker you're in the spotlight. You're offering your opinion to an audience, sharing your expertise and hopefully sharing a new perspective or idea. I definitely know going into any presentation that approximately 10-20% of the crowd will not like me. And they shouldn't. Because if they did – it means I'm not stirring the pot enough.

One thing I didn't count on when I got into the business was how you occasionally get the *zinger* comment from people who have nothing better to do.

I've heard them all…and the funny thing is…it's never about the content!

Here's a few: (If you said this to me – look sweetheart– you're famous now!)

- I like your hair better the other way/other color
- I see the Diva has finally put some Junk in her Trunk
- Kim, did you know you have a zit on your neck?

- You don't look at all like your book cover – your cover has cheek bones
- Loved your speech, but I could see where your nylons ended
- I WOULD NEVER put those 2 colors together

Eesh.

It definitely can be a challenge when YOU are the one they're calling *The Ugly Baby*. You can feel like you're in a boxing ring!

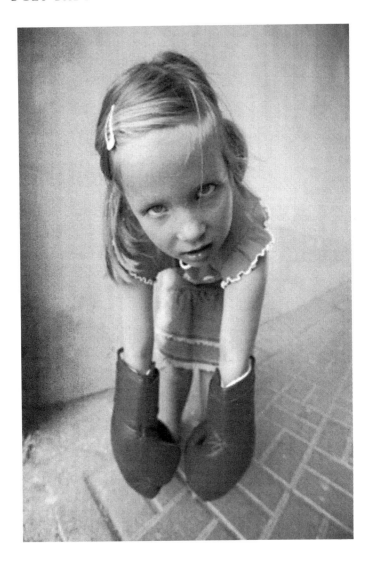

However – I love this quote from Fanny Flagg and so should you:

> "If people are talking about you behind your back, It's only because you're in the front."

Love that one! (So they can all look at my so-called panty line as much as they want. Enjoy the view, baby!)

So what off-sets those negative people and comments? (Who really are just a tiny handful)

All the other kazillion wonderful people who thank me for putting myself out there, not following the crowd, taking chances and speaking from my heart.

It adds to the magic invisible bubble I imagine around myself when I see an Energy Vampire approaching. Energy Vampires are attracted to positive people — especially those who *they secretly envy*.

How do you know they are Energy Vampires? They have a steel glint in their eye (they always say something "fake-nice" first) and then ZAP they hit you with what they hope will kill your confidence and shake your game.

But BOING — the magic bubble bounces their garbage right back at them and I go have a piece of cake to add to the "junk in my trunk."

When someone criticizes your idea in a not-so-very-nice way, the best thing to do is smile, look them right in the eye and say "That's interesting feedback" and then move on.

(In the speaking world it's called The California Blow-Off)

Then distance yourself from the little lonely soul-sucking vampire freak as soon as you can.

I learned this from one of my mentors - Oprah.

When I hit the treadmill I watch the Special DVD set of Oprah's 25 Years which highlights some of the best and worst shows Oprah experienced.

One of the most enlightening stories is about an **Ugly Baby** moment she had with a world famous actress.

Oprah speaks about the first interview she did with Elizabeth Taylor. Oprah was thrilled and nervous to be interviewing her as she had admired her from afar for many years.

Just before they were starting to tape the interview – Elizabeth Taylor looked at Oprah with those dazzling violet eyes and said something to the effect of:

"I don't want you to ask me any questions of my life before today"

Cameras rolling!

Oprah said she could not believe what had just happened and it was the longest, most tortuous interview of her life.

So she put on her frozen smile and went on with the show…even though Elizabeth Taylor in no uncertain terms, was calling her and her show an *Ugly Baby*.

When you watch the clip you can absolutely feel the tension in the air and Oprah is struggling but still pressing forward. She is being sooooo nice to Elizabeth Taylor (who quite frankly didn't deserve it) and you can tell Oprah is swallowing all the questions she's had building inside of her for years.

She must have needed a GIANT antacid after the interview.

I thought it took guts for Oprah to reveal the video clip of her *Ugly Baby* moment to the world AND to also describe her vulnerable emotions behind the scenes as well.

So remember -if it can happen to Oprah it can happen to you too.

And also remember it speaks more about THEM than it does YOU.

I think this whimsical and wise poem captures the hazards of listening to others TOO much:

E D
- BY LOUIS SIMPSON

Ed was in love with a cocktail waitress,
but Ed's family, and his friends,
didn't approve. So he broke it off.

He married a respectable woman
who played the piano. She played well enough
to have been a professional.

Ed's wife left him …
Years later, at a family gathering
Ed got drunk and made a fool of himself.

He said, "I should have married Doreen."
"Well," they said, "why didn't you?"

So listen.

Don't be an Ed.

BUT REMEMBER – BE OPEN TO CONSTRUCTIVE CRITICISM

Now this is a tough one. You have to be willing to take medicine that's good for you! (Even if initially it tastes as nasty as Buckley's cough syrup.)

(In case you're not a Canadian … Buckley's is the nastiest, foulest, worst-tasting, pine-tar-mixed-with-goat-urine–and-gasoline–and-a-side-shot–of-ear wax -tasting cough syrup. But it works. It literally scares the cold right out of you.)

In business, you have to be willing to filter out the comments meant to unhinge you in a cruel way from the comments that are helpful in an observational way.

Initially they can both feel the same.

So how do you do this?

Use your gut feeling and instincts plus with a healthy dose of logic thrown in! Learn to separate the two by trusting your gut feeling about the people who are giving you feedback as well as their credibility.

Feedback can be a weird thing.

You have to take everything with a grain of salt — from both the positive and negative.

You can have someone rave about what you do and your idea— but if they are too close to you, they think you're wonderful no matter what you do! (Family members, spouses, friends, some competitors and your drooling Dalmatian definitely fall into this category)

You can also have someone at the other end of the spectrum who is negative by being direct and rude and or in a passive-aggressive way. (Family members, spouses, friends, some competitors and your miserable cat definitely fall into THIS category!)

Listen, lady   Be careful who you share your idea with.

Years ago I wrote a manuscript on growing up in a small town. I also wrote the series of stories in the voice of a 10-year old girl.

I made the amateur mistake of showing the manuscript to a friend who wanted to read it. I'll never forget this image – I was driving up to my garage and I could see her in my back yard reading the manuscript. That was great! (I was secretly thrilled!)

She never did write anything in the manuscript or say *one word* to me about it. She didn't need to. I could tell simply by her body language that she was upset for some reason. Good or bad -she never said one word about it.

And I could feel all those *Ugly Baby* vibes coming at me through the picket fence.

It was a harsh lesson. You have to be very careful about WHEN and TO WHOM you should first run past your idea. I call it my "virgin author experience" where you're looking for affirmation in all the wrong places. And it applies to every situation when you're launching new ideas and not just books.

This was a completely different experience from another friend who read the manuscript with a critical yet loving eye. And yes – she's a writer, reads voraciously and her constructive criticism helped take the book to a whole new level.

Another cherished friend of mine is a screenwriter in Hollywood. He actually asked me to send him the manuscript and I kept postponing doing it (oh yeah – I was worried about the **Ugly Baby** and especially since he's SUCH a talented writer).

Because really. He's written for television shows like the X-Files, Frasier, and wrote a movie for Robin Williams…. he's SUPER GOOD! (Although only I know as a kid he was afraid of television sets. Yep.)

So I finally grew a backbone instead of a wishbone and I sent him the story. I thought I was going to throw up when I gave the package to the lady at the post office.

And he read it and sent it back. Tons of red slash marks – paragraphs crossed out, questions peppered through-out.

And yet.
And yet.
And yet.

It made all the difference and I could SEE how the manuscript would be transformed simply because of his ideas. He also had acknowledged everything I had done right and where I was on track.

IT GAVE ME HOPE.

And that's the kind of constructive criticism you want. The kind that will make you shine.

Remember – constructive criticism is just that. This feedback isn't intended to hurt you. Instead the intent is to help you in any way possible and to offer an unbiased perspective. It should give you a sense of *hopefulness*.

If it doesn't – then someone is trying to carve you and your idea for dinner. And even though you may feel like a turkey sometimes, you don't deserve that.

So ask yourself these questions. And I want you to REALLY think about this!

Who are you currently allowing to give you feedback? Why?
Why is their opinion important to you?
Who doesn't want you to succeed? (and deep down you know it)
Who wants to see you fly to the stars with success?
What are you planning on doing with their feedback?
Can you handle NOT being right? (That means wrong by the way!)
Will you be able to take criticism from this person?
Are they someone who understands your target customer?
Are they someone who understands your goals?
Do they have ANY CREDIBILITY in this area?

LEARN FROM THE TELEVISION NETWORKS!

Something I learned years ago working in national television is when you have a large database to tap into — one letter or phone call stands for many. It's all about the percentages.

If someone actually took the time to write a letter to the station about their concern over a commercial or a program — it was taken seriously.

Why?

Because for every person who wrote a letter they knew thousands of other television viewers felt the same way but were never going to write in.

The key phrase here is "large database".

When you're asking and receiving feedback on your idea remember to look at the percentages.

1. How large is your customer database?
2. Is this person your target audience?

Also — don't drive the bus of your business based on what a small number of people have to say — unless those people have MASSIVE CREDIBILITY for you!

Absolutely do not make decisions based on opinions of people who will never be a customer or use your idea in any way, shape or form. Plus – how SUCCESSFUL are they in their own ventures? (Usually the most criticizing people are the ones who have the least amount of success and courage.)

Sometimes you'll see in an article (or something in Prevention magazine) about a health remedy that's not being taken seriously. It's because the Sample Survey was too small, not for a long enough period of time, or wasn't tested on the people it would be intended for.

Your idea is the same, lady!

You don't offer your best recipe for chocolate cake, which you want to be the headliner in your new bakery, to some-one who hates chocolate or who hates cake or hates dessert. It just wouldn't make sense now would it??

So if you're serious about launching your new idea and you're willing to take the chances of it being called an *Ugly Baby* – then you MUST take a smart, proactive approach to getting feedback.

Remember – you don't want to have the same "Virgin Author" approach as I did all those years ago! Your idea shouldn't be pitched in front of people who aren't a match in the first place.

SO HOW CAN YOU BE OH-SO-PRO-ACTIVE AND SMART?

You're going to survey your customers.

And not just in ANY old way. Nope.

You want to listen to the wise words of Mary Lou Quinlan, CEO and founder of Just Ask A Woman in New York city.

In her book, with the same title as her company – Just Ask A Woman – she talks about one of the fundamental mistakes made in doing focus-testing:

"About eight to ten women show up at a dreary building in a nondescript mall, fill in more answers on a clipboard, and warily eye the other women in the waiting room. Eventually, they file back to a windowless, fluorescent-lit room (the most unflattering lighting for women, by the way) to sit in hard chairs at a Formica conference table adorned with cans of warm soda and bowls of stale chips. A moderator who is probably tired from completing earlier groups on deodorants or insurance greets them. She invites them to relax for casual conversation about a subject such as incontinence with the following caveats. She professes to have nothing to do with the ideas that they are about to discuss, and she reveals that the room is bugged with hidden recording devices and that a two-way mirror conceals other people who are watching, even though the women can't see them."

You have to read the rest of this story in Mary Lou's book as it absolutely cracked me up when I first read it! Years ago when I worked in television advertising, I actually attended a focus group for a client just like the example above – except I was one of the people behind the two-way mirror!

It is exactly as she describes and of course – the feedback is totally meaningless.

So don't do that. And don't pay a fortune for getting feedback regarding your idea.

You can ask an association to run it past their members, give out samples with an incentive to give you feedback anonymously, or ask someone else to interview people so they don't have to worry about hurting your feelings etc.

There are tons of methods to ask for feedback you can use, to not only alter your idea…but it will probably give you loads of new dazzling ideas as well!

RESOURCES FOR SURVEYING YOUR CUSTOMERS AND POTENTIAL CUSTOMERS:

1. www.surveymonkey.com
2. www.askmydatabase.com
3. www.surveygizmo.com

SO HOW'S YOUR MAGICAL, INVISIBLE BUBBLE DOING?

Years ago there was a TV show called "Get Smart". Maxwell Smart and his boss would enter the "Dome of Silence" Your magical bubble is like that – and it helps you from becoming too thick-skinned, cynical, jaded, defensive and bitter when people call your idea an *Ugly Baby*.

Remember lady – there are worse things than having an *Ugly Baby*.

What, you may ask?

The worst would be if you NEVER brought your idea to the world.

That would be the Ugliest Baby of all.

CHAPTER EIGHT:

Her Podcasts Attract Millions Of People!

I love the synchronicity of life.

Out of the blue I received an email one day – a woman named Karen Luniw – she had found me on the internet somehow and wanted to connect. She was an entrepreneur who was using podcasting as a means of spreading the word about her website www.karenluniw.com.

Karen had recently left the corporate world to jump into her own business.

She didn't have much money to promote her business so she decided to do it as creatively and inexpensively as possible – by uploading her podcasts to iTunes (which is FREE by the way!) Karen doesn't believe in whining about what she doesn't have – she jumps into what she creates. And boy-oh-boy did this lady create success.

Except Karen wasn't just having ordinary success with the podcasts – she was having extraordinary success!

We absolutely connected on the phone and being a former media girl – I encouraged Karen to send a news release to the media – promoting her recent success: She was one of the Top 20 podcasts on iTunes in the world. Yes – she was right up there with Oprah! (I kid you not)

I helped her write a news release and the rest is history. Karen was interviewed by the majority of the Canadian national media and has since been approached by a major national book publisher and she's receiving speaking gigs on cruises!

There's so much to learn from Karen so let's jump right into our interview, your brain will never be the same (and neither will your business for that matter).

Plus you'll be salivating to start your own podcast. Wear a bib!

UGLY BABY INTERVIEW:

Karen Luniw

www.karenluniw.com

Kim:	What made you decide to get into law of attraction? Were you working for another company at that time or please share?
Karen:	I'd been in the employment industry for more years then I care to say (over 20 years!)

My theory is always that nobody should be in this business more than 5 years and 20 years later I was still there. The thing was I got better at what I did, as then I got to work with staff which is what I really like to do. And so and then, of course, there's more money and it's pretty convenient to stay and you just get wrapped up in it.

Kim: **I call it the golden handcuffs!**

Karen: What ended up happening is 10 years ago I decided I really wanted to make a break and found coaching and wanted to start my own business and have an internet presence way back then. That's when I first came across law of attraction - probably about 10 or 12 years ago.

I started studying it and teaching people and coaching people. I had my business for a short period of time but then went back into the corporate world. But always kept the law of attraction and was working it with clients and staff and saw how it worked and didn't work for people. So it's just always been there for me. I've been a really avid student of it for a long time now.

Of course, it wasn't well known back then and if you tried to Google it and this was even in the days before Google you couldn't even...

Kim: People would think "Like law of attraction? What are you even talking about here? Is it about sex?"

Karen: Exactly! And people always said is this a dating service or something? Well no but boy that would probably make a lot of money. So that's where the law of attraction came from. I've studied it through a variety of people, most notably Abraham Hicks.

Karen: So then when I heard The Secret came out I thought NOW is the time to act. I'd always had an interest in internet marketing and I wanted to have a presence and I'd discovered podcasting as well. The time was just right.

Kim: So before you decided to do that big old scary leap where you went from living in the world of the corporate environment to going out on your own, what did you go through? Did you talk to people about it? What were your friends and family and everybody saying and also who you worked with, what did they think of you doing this?

Karen: They think it's awesome. They just think it was the next thing for me. I've been really fortunate in the fact that I've had lots of really, really supportive people around me. I think if my dad was alive he probably would have been pulling his hair out. He always said to me "get a government job Karen, OK?"

Kim: **That's very old school and that's how everyone was taught, focus on security vs joy. Did you leave your job right away?**

Karen: No- I launched my podcast in December 2006 and people started downloading right away, which was quite amazing to me. I put it up on iTunes and in the first month I think I had 18,000 downloads and the month after was more and it just kept building to the point where I was getting about 30,000 downloads a month.

After about 6 months, it was around 120,000 downloads I had by that point and the emails I would get from people all over the world just saying "wow this is just great, thank you you've helped me so much." It was just very gratifying.

So when you have a staff of 15 as opposed to people all over the world who you really feel like you're helping it was like... I need a bigger audience then my staff, right??? I was ready to leave my job.

Kim: **What was your last day at your job like? So many people who are reading this are going to be going through all sorts of different life transitions. They're deciding they're going to start a new business, or maybe they're deciding they want to travel around the world for a year but they're sitting on the cusp and that's why they'll be reading Ugly Baby going "I need some kind of nudge to get rid of the "scared" feelings I have."**

Karen:　　My husband has transitioned through jobs a lot and he's been great and every time he's done that he's gone on to something different and even better. He's just enjoyed that. I was complaining or talking my talk about my work and he said, "Karen - if you don't quit your job I'm going to quit and you're going to have to stay there forever."

Kim:　　**I love it! Now how is that for a stiletto in the butt?**

Karen:　　Oh my God and honestly it sent me into a panic because I thought he was serious. I thought "No way, this is my time!" and so I don't never really get like this but I j was completely anxious all day long because it's all about the security. I had a paycheck, I was getting paid well. How am I going to pay my bills? Where is it all going to come from? I just couldn't figure it out.

　　　　　　Then by midday I thought I could take a leave of absence. I'm going to take a leave of absence and use some of my holidays and take the summer off.

Karen: So I phoned Jeff later that afternoon and told him about my idea. He had absolutely no intention of quitting his job and he said "Oh that's great. Good for you!"

Kim: **It was a nice little cattle prod for you!**

Karen: Yes! I took the two months off - July and August and I came back after the September long weekend and I had a great summer. I worked really hard in my own business and created a booklet for sale and got a really great response that paid for my time off that I wasn't being paid for by the company. I was kind of hoping somehow, some way somebody would lay me off when I got back!

I just really didn't know what I was going to do when I came back. I kept thinking "We'll just see, maybe it's not that bad" and 2 hours into it, my boss and I and I love her, I enjoyed her so much and we had lots of fun at work, she was just so happy to have me back and she said "I've basically booked up your whole September." And 2 hours into it I just thought, "Oh my God I can't do it, I can't do it."

I phoned her and we met later that afternoon and she pulled up, we met at Starbucks, and she pulled up and said, "you're quitting aren't you?" I said, "Yes- I can't do it!" She knew when I left on my holiday- she just knew I wasn't going to come back. So everybody else knew it but I didn't!

Kim: **Isn't that funny and that can happen can't it - that other people have clarity about what is right for you but we're so close to ourselves, we're so close to the situation. It's like you have your nose standing up against the wall and you need the perspective.**

Karen: It really came down to security. I just couldn't imagine giving up my security of my job and the dollars coming in... for I had no clue what!

Kim: **Isn't that interesting even just the whole word security. We were always** taught and I was taught this as well, that it's an outside influence that creates it for us, when in fact it is exactly the opposite. That security is absolutely an internally created emotion. I tell many, many women entrepreneurs that I work with around the world and they'll be just like you were and I was before I left my big fat corporate job in television. And they'll just say "How about if I'm a bag lady pushing a cart down the street with a bunch of cats wrapped around my neck?" I always say to them "Okay look in your life has that ever happened to you? Have you ever been on the street? Have you never had a roof over your head?" Most people they go "No I've never had that."

So it's like "well then why would you start now?" Your natural place is of abundance and of growth and everything else. What's the great quote from Henry David Thoreau? He said "May you love your discontent because it means you're on the cusp of growth."

Karen: Oh that's wonderful!

**Kim: So whenever you're feeling in that
            painful weird little place that's what
            it is. So that's why I just love what
            you did. So you told your boss at
            Starbucks who did support you even
            though she is panicking and thinking
            "How in the hell am I going to get all
            this work done without Karen?" So
            what was the next step for you?**

Karen: I gave a month's notice and it was quick
            because they were all going "Are you
            sure you don't want to go before?" Not
            that they didn't want me around, it was
            just I couldn't be as useful to them as
            they needed me to because they didn't
            want to involve me back with staff
            again. It was just like "Karen- just get
            on with it and go do what you need to
            do; this is the right thing for you to do."

            I worked my month out and on the
            Thanksgiving long weekend I left
            and celebrated and just really decom-
            pressed after that and it took a while.

Kim: It does take time to get back in that place. Well… it's almost a new head space! It's like "Wow-NOW I'm an entrepreneur!"

Karen: Yes totally!

Kim: Now I know all about the success of your podcast and the unbelievable fame you are attracting to yourself but please share this with the people who will be reading Ugly Baby. Tell us what has been happening, so we know that first year, only a year ago and you had 120,000 downloads. Where are you sitting today Karen?

Karen: Kim-you're just such a funny catalyst in my life because as of this point I have 12 million downloads!

Kim: The hairs just stood up on the back of my neck! I'm so proud of you. From one Canadian to another you rock!

Karen: Thank you!

Kim: Everybody reading this —Karen has had 12 million downloads. Do you realize that's bigger than the city of New York? Again, she was just working in a normal corporate job just like so many of us have done and with a little bit of ingenuity and trying something new this is what has come out of it. It's absolutely brilliant.

Kim: I'm going to move into your big brain here, what would be something if you could go back in time and do again what would you do? Is there anything that you wish "Oh I shouldn't have done that?"

Karen: A few years ago, I lost my email list. I had not set it up properly so my internet service provider shut me down when I was sending out to my list. I do a weekly tips letter on the law of attraction and they were sending it out. I was actually about to promote a teleclass coming up that was going to be my big money maker for the beginning of the year and I was shut down.

So if I would have done anything differently? I would have done what I was told to do in the first place, which was use a list host instead of using my own computer. So that is one thing I would have done for sure!

Kim: **So then you would still have all those people in your database.**

Karen: Yes and now the cool thing is I made back my list already in 6 months which took me a year to make before. So that's really neat. I don't know if there is anything else. I could say that I would have left my job earlier but I just don't think the timing would have been right.

I went through a number of trials and tribulations. It hasn't been all roses and after that list, I let my list kind of fall away from me and it was like "okay I no longer have a business. I had a business and now I have nothing so what does that mean?" So what it helped me to do was look in a different direction

and start to get a little bit more creative about where I was going.

So I came up with some different ideas,
so as kind of painful as those moments
are, like you just said about the Thoreau
comment...just out of those dark moments comes the most amazing things.

Kim: **What would you recommend women
do? What would be some of the things
that you would say if someone is reading this interview and it's a year from
now or a couple of years from now,
they've found this fabulous book about
ideas called Ugly Baby and now they're
reading the Kim Duke and Karen
Luniw interview and they read these
words and it propels them like a rock-
et launch. What would you tell them?**

Karen: I keep forging ahead and give myself
permission to be me and that is okay.
And I don't have to do it the old boys
way, I don't have to do it like a man, I
don't have to be in business and act like
a man, I don't have to be a man.

I think it really is coming down to giving yourself permission to be who you are and to really follow those little nigglies inside of you that point you in a direction where you say "I can't do that" or "this isn't right" or "who is going to listen to me" is to get over it and go forward anyway.

Kim: **Isn't a big part of law of attraction (because I'm a big fan of the whole philosophy) is that sometimes we need some contrast to be able to see what we do want in life? I don't like turnips, well hey maybe you would like carrots instead? I know I'm really simplifying it but that's kind of the way it is, that's how we learn what we do like and what we do want.**

Karen: Absolutely and I break the law of attraction down into 5 steps and the first step really is know what you don't want and giving yourself permission to not like some things and not like to do some of those things that you might do just because you think you're supposed to do them. So give yourself permission not to do them and then figure out, my 2nd step is to figure out what it is you do want and really again give yourself permission to do that.

Again, as women we really are caretakers and that's part of what we've grown up with and so we're always looking after others but not necessarily looking after our own best interests at the same time. We're trying to be everything to everybody else and not really being ourselves.

Karen: It comes down to I had lots of doubts but every moment when I came back to "Maybe I just have to go get a job" there were many fibers of my being that screamed out "No, no, no!" and so I've just gone forward and acted on those inspirations and those moments where I feel I have to make a phone call to somebody specifically at that moment or fire off an email at the right time. Those are the things that have made the difference.

Kim: **Karen — make sure to remember me when you're sitting across from Oprah!**

So,

An ordinary woman leaves her ordinary big-money corporate job because she wants to create a business about Law of Attraction. Not so ordinary NOW is it?

Sounds like it had lots of Ugly Baby potential! But Karen Luniw went ahead and did it anyway and now she has millions of people listening to her podcasts.

She's someone just like you.

Psssssssssssssssst.

Want to know something we forgot to tell you in this interview?

Karen records the podcasts IN HER CLOSET with her computer! Yes – right in there with her dresses, jeans, shoes and laundry basket Karen is creating a business that's making her a WHOLE lot of money.

Why the closet? (Honestly, I cracked up when she first shared this with me!)

She likes the sound of it on her podcast. I think she feels like she's in her own Secret Garden creating magic for the world! (and if you haven't read THAT book get thee to a bookstore!)

Who says you have to follow the rules??

CHAPTER NINE:

Is Your Idea "Spreadable"?

In order for your idea to succeed it has to be "spreadable."

Don't laugh, lady.

Your idea will die a dramatic soap-opera death if other people don't spread the word for you.

So think of yourself as a **giant, beautiful butter pat** you want your customers and target customers to SPREAD on their friends, co-workers, on Facebook and other social media, and to anyone else who would be a perfect fit for you. (P.S. and these people LOVE IT)

Sounds kinky but it's not!

BUTTER ME UP BABY!

The term "viral marketing" was coined a few years ago, but in my experience, when women hear the word VIRAL they think:

Yuck!

Why?

Well they think of:

- wiping their kids nose and getting up 5 times a night for 2 weeks
- the guy who sneezed on them on the subway (the one with the really bad teeth)

- the 8 hours they spent in an emergency room after eating at the wonderful, all-you-can-eat cheap buffet place with the shag carpet
- sore throats, runny or stuffed noses, puffy eyes and overall ugliness
- when chocolate is impossible to taste (travesty!)
- when they were sick as a dog, went to the store with chapped lips, nose and scary sweatpants and bumped into their hot, old boy-friend.

I say to hell with viral.

Let's just spray some extra strength disinfectant on the phrase VIRAL MARKETING and knock it back into its slimy, bug-filled world.

Instead we'll re-invent it and call it something fresh, something we all adore, something we as women do as easily as breathing, multi-tasking and trying new mascara.

Let's call it......

GOOD GOSSIP!

Let's chat about this for a minute. (Because THAT's what good gossipers DO)

Maybe as a kid you were taught gossip was a bad thing. (I know I certainly was!) And your mom was right. (I know how much you love hearing that.)

Any gossip that's negative, untrue, hurtful etc is never acceptable under any circumstances.

However, I'm not talking about that nastiness. And this is what your mom neglected to tell you.

NOT ALL GOSSIP that flies is like the wicked witch of the west.

I'm challenging the miserable washed-up theory of gossip. Right here, right now.

Because I think GOSSIP can be something incredibly powerful, incredibly positive and it can accelerate your business to levels you haven't even dreamed of yet.

I call it GOOD GOSSIP.

I grew up in a small town that had an even smaller general store. Tons of people from the town and surrounding community would drive in each morning and get their mail, have a cup of coffee on "Coffee Row" and connect with each other.

My dad would always ask my mom at lunch:

"So—did you hear any GOOD GOSSIP?"

SO WHAT DOES GOOD GOSSIP DO?

It connects people.

It spreads the word about great products and services, people and ideas.

It creates common ground between strangers.

It allows sharing.

It's helpful, uplifting and positive.

It's fun!

Don't even try to tell me that you don't gossip.

I don't believe you.

I know you gossip.

I do it too.

In fact, I'm not sure I could live without it!

You're gossiping about all sorts of snazzy things, lady:

- Where you got your new jeans that don't create muffin top
- The facial cream you swear has peeled off 10 years and 1 ex- husband
- The new hair stylist who gave you a new and sexy look
- The best baby-sitter on the block (she even puts the dishes away!)
- The salad recipe that made every one moan at the table with delight

- The banker who gave you a loan without making you feel like a beggar
- The restaurant with the BEST bathroom (honest – you have to see it!)
- This cool hotel you stayed at on your vacation
- The car dealer who treated you like royalty
- The best farmer's market in the city
- Which networking association doesn't ask for referrals like they were Halloween candy
- Where you bought those **fabuloussssss shoes**

And the list goes on and on!

You're gossiping about so many positive people, places, products and services, businesses, ideas, gadgets, techniques and strategies EVERY DAY it's almost impossible to keep track of.

Where oh where do you find the time??

Have you ever promoted a business, or person you loved? Of course you have.

And it wasn't difficult either! In fact, when we're excited about something it is a JOY to spread the word to others…we can hardly wait to share!

This is exactly WHY your idea has to be plugged into The Good Gossip Network.

A perfect example of this is my lovely and wonderful friend Jo-ann.

She was visiting for the week-end, and we sat in front of the fire, sipping wine and catching up.

Jo said:

"Hey – have you the Neutrogena micro dermabrasion kit? It's a little vibrating machine with a soft pad – you put this cream on it with little crystals – and you rub it all over your face. You do it every day for a week – I can't believe how wonderful my skin feels!"

Then she said (it still makes me laugh as I type this):

"I just lovvvvvvvvve the feeling of all those little cuts on my face —
I can tell my wrinkles are disappearing!"

Jo is the Skin Queen so anything she says – I'm buying!

A few days later I had another good friend come over for coffee.

And you guessed it. I said …

"Hey Tina, have you heard about the Neutrogena micro dermabrasion kit? It's a little vibrating machine with a soft pad – you put this cream on it with little crystals – and you rub it all over your face. You do it every day for a week – my friend Jo says she can't believe how wonderful her skin feels!"

Tina and I looked at each other.

She said... *"Let's GO!"*

We jumped in the car and drove to the nearest large drug store and sure enough – there was Jo's masterpiece. We not only bought the little vibrating face machines – we also bought a ton of the replacement pads and cream (they were 50% off don't you know)

Here's what's so interesting about this. We didn't:

- See one magazine ad
- Hear a radio commercial
- Go to a tradeshow
- Get a sample in the mail
- Find out on Oprah
- Have someone cold call us

But we still went out and purchased $200 worth of stuff because of what MY FRIEND SAID – and Tina doesn't even know her!

That's called plugging into the Good Gossip Network.

SO WHAT IS THE GOOD GOSSIP NETWORK?

Imagine a spider web.

It's intricate, delicate and connected in a myriad of ways.
It's powerful, flexible and beautiful.
And often overlooked.

Women DON'T get stuck in the web.

Instead we can run nimbly from one section to the other, just like the lovely little spider Charlotte in Charlotte's web, mending, creating, sharing, adding and testing as needed.

When a Good Piece of Gossip lands in the web – it sends vibrations immediately, and very quickly the people who need to know…ARE IN THE KNOW. (And remember – women know an average of 250 people)

As you're reading this, I'm sure a million things are crossing your mind.

You're probably remembering…

- All of the times you've told a friend about something new
- All of the times you've heard from a friend about something you didn't know

The Good Gossip Network is based upon sharing information with others – so they move from NOT KNOWING – to KNOWING.

And because the information is so valuable, it gains speed and momentum and WHOOSH you are plugged into the Good Gossip Network!

So whether you know it or not – our world is run by Good Gossip. Now what's YOUR message to the world, Charlotte?

AN AMERICAN IN PARIS MAKING SUNDAY DINNER?

I'm a traveler. Travelers are always on the hunt for new places to go, food to try and new people to meet. Our Good Gossip radar is on 24-7.

Each week my ezine subscribers/Facebook/Twitter from over 54 countries receives sales tips, articles etc and also what I'm up to. I mentioned to them I was headed to Paris. The ideas flowed in! Fabulous recommendations of what to do, what to avoid and I NOW know where the world's best baguettes and pain au chocolat are made!

The Good Gossip Network was really fired up about my trip. And of course, through a friend of a friend of a friend…I received a link about www.jim-haynes.com Jim is a 70+ old guy who's lived in Paris for almost 40 years.

What's so unusual about Jim? He's been holding Sunday Dinners for travelers (or anyone for that matter) at his Parisian apartment for over 30 years!!

Jim's soirees are famous in Paris and beyond. He's been interviewed by almost every major television and radio network in the world as well as several international magazines and newspapers.

Why? Because what he's doing is SPREADABLE.

You book ahead (and I mean far ahead) to attend a Sunday Dinner. You receive the code to get into the verdant courtyard of Jim's atelier and all the food and cheap wine you want.

International travelers (just like me) pay ONLY $25 Euro each to have all the food and wine they want and of course enjoy incredible conversation out in the beautiful courtyard as well as in Jim's eclectic and book-filled apartment.

In Paris - Jim is incredibly famous for his soirees and he has a different chef each week. In fact, chefs from all over the world volunteer to cook for him each week (how cool!) I met the most incredible people from Paris, London, Australia, California, Holland and beyond...everyone was chatting in the courtyard, drinking wine and having

fun! I've made new friends and business connections....
and the BEST part? I actually met one of my favorite
authors Veronique Vienne (what a thrill! She's written
several books and for Vogue and the New York Times to
name a few.)

When I was at the soiree, there were almost 70 people
from all over the world. Here's what is so cool. Everyone had found out about Jim ONLY through word of
mouth or by his media coverage. I interviewed him for
my blog while he perched his lanky frame on a kitchen
stool – obviously soaking up all the attention of the people around him.

He doesn't spend a dime on advertising. Because he's pro-
viding people with an incredible experience, an opportunity for people from every country imaginable to meet with
each other, share conversation, wine and food…his idea is
spreadable and has been doing so for over 30 years so far.

Remember – no advertising. The next time you go to
Paris – look him up.

I want you to devote a good chunk of time and thinking
to HOW your idea can become a Good Gossip topic.

Why waste time, money and energy trying to sell your idea
to one person at a time YOURSELF…when instead – you
can plug into the Good Gossip Network and sell your idea
to HUNDREDS, THOUSANDS and beyond?

You have a choice really.

You can spend a fortune doing it the hard way.

Or you can be smart about it, and put your time, money and effort into being REMARKABLE. Be strategic about getting into the Good Gossip Network.

HOW STARBUCKS BECAME THE TALK OF THE TOWN

Several years ago Starbucks did some Good Gossiping on purpose.

They didn't advertise. They didn't have big billboards. They didn't do anything except….

Tell customers they were giving away Grande Frappacinos for FREE -ALL DAY at certain locations.

My sister called me at home and left messages. About 10,001 times. Now of course, today, we'd be slapping it on Facebook and Twitter in 3 seconds.

"Kim-you MUST head to Starbucks! Heather just called – she told me about their Frappacino day – I took the girls and YES – they are really giving away Grande Frappacinos of your choice!"

Of course I went! Any writer worth their salt has part of their DNA embedded in a Starbucks chair. And yessss – I took my nieces and you bet – we walked out of there with creamcicle frappacinos and big smiles.

Now before you think *"What a waste of money – Starbucks wouldn't have sold those customers anything else that day…no one would be thirsty."*

Um. You need to give your head a shake, sister.

175

Instead of paying $10,000 for a full page ad in a newspaper for one day – (and that's for a small city with a million people) Starbucks plugged into the Good Gossip Network. Women, men, little children and grannies spread the word for free for them. And it probably only cost them pennies per serving.

What would you rather do?

Spend money on advertising with no guarantee of success? Or promote something to your database of customers who love you, reward them, create some excitement and fun, reinforce the relationship and loyalty, create an intense positive memory, and also **CREATE BUZZ** that probably would hit the media and have people talking about Starbucks for weeks?

Yeah – I think they probably made a fortune from that day of Free Frapps and the ripple effect is probably still happening.

Some Secrets to Starbucks success?

1. **They didn't cheap out.** They didn't offer little rinky-dinky sized cups for free as that wouldn't have created any buzz. And they knew it takes a lot of ice, syrup and cream before you spend $20,000.

2. **They didn't give-away hotdogs or pancakes in a parking lot.** Because boy-oh-boy — waiting in a long line-up to get a cheap burnt hotdog or a doughy pancake certainly makes me jump into my car (how about you?)

3. **The baristas were pumped**. They weren't sullen and grouchy because they had tons of people rolling in. They were laughing and were just as excited as the customers. I still remember their refreshing attitude!

You'll discover the women I interviewed for this book definitely have something worth talking about. They've been "Frapped".

They get it.

They are innovative, unique, daring to be bold, and they have worked very hard at "becoming spreadable!"

Do you currently have an idea/product/business/service that's worth telling the world about? If not — tap into the feedback customers and potential customers can give you.

They'll tell you. They'll help you. And before you know it — you'll be on your way through the good gossip "web".

I double-dog dare you.

CHAPTER TEN:

Create Your Community of Raving Fans

OK - I'm a grown woman and can admit this.

I'm a RAVING FAN of Sex And The City! (re-runs and all) I'll be an 80-year old woman who will still be dreaming about Mr. Big. Sigh.

When the first movie came out -I saw it with a ton of my girlfriends (I even wore a poofy skirt and leopard stilettos) and we had a ball! (And don't tell anyone – but I own the 6-season set, the movies, the sound tracks and the cheesy game as well)

"You put high heels on and you change."

-Manolo Blahnik

And YES -I was one of the die-hards who loved the HBO show as soon as it launched years ago and I definitely helped spread the word of Carrie, Samantha, Charlotte and Miranda. (And we can't forget about Biggggggggggggggggg. Heavy sigh.)

I'm not the only one.

Millions of fans (many of whom came from watching the syndicated re-runs) ran anxiously in their 3-inch stilettos to shell out their hard-earned cash for the movie.

You had to love the frenzy!

THE BIG SALES LESSON YOU CAN LEARN FROM SEX AND THE CITY?

Oh and this is BIG.

What did a little HBO television show that was only on air for 6 years (and barely scraped through the first 3 seasons by the way) do to garner such attention?

It turned women (and many men) into RAVING FANS.

How?

Although it was **different, risky, often shocking...what it did best** was portray female friendships.

It absolutely resonated with the hearts and minds of every woman who has ever dated a dud with small hands and bad breath or struggled with finding her way in this world. And who then shared her struggles and bad dates over bacon, eggs and coffee with her girlfriends.

You can never say Sex and The City played it safe and didn't take chances. You may love or hate the show but what you can't deny is THE POWER OF THEIR FANS.

Heck - I even went on a cheesy tour when I was in New York (and yes - I was on Carrie's steps of her brownstone) and yes, I even had the over-rated, over-icing-ed $5.00 cupcake at the Magnolia Bakery.

Why? I'm a fan.

Let me ask you something about what you do.

Do you have fans? Does your idea have potential for fans?

Does Your "Fan Club"...

- help **spread the word** about your business for free?
- notice you're **taking some chances** and launching new products and services?
- supply you with ideas on how to **grow** your business?
- hear from you on a **regular basis** - via an e-zine, event, direct mail and the phone and through social media?
- buy everything (or almost everything) you put in front of them because they **TRUST** you so much?

If so - then congratulations! If not - then lady - you have some work to do!

Creating a community of fans is the BEST thing you can do to grow your sales. It takes time, hard work and dedication to rising above the HUMDRUM.

Instead of putting all that time into cold calling strangers - how about speaking to the people who already love you? And then ASK THEM to tell people about you- make it EASY for them to SHARE YOU (which they'll do anyway if they love what you do) Back to the Good Gossip Network theme! (and of course, social media is one of the best FREE places for this to happen)

I think you can see the connection can't you?

SEX AND THE CITY GETS IT AND ALWAYS DID

Remember - you are your VERY own version of Carrie, Samantha, Miranda and Charlotte.

And it's possible for YOU TOO to have a group of fans for your idea.

So whatcha waiting for, lady??

"Do it trembling, if you must, but do it."

- Emmett Fox

*I really like that trembling part.

I wanted to include unusual examples of developing a community and I hit the history books for this next one! You know all about social media but I bet you didn't know about THIS.

ONLY THE TOP SALESPEOPLE IN THE WORLD BAKE THIS STRATEGY – DO YOU??

No matter what your idea is – there's something I know for sure.

At some point in your life (maybe even as you're reading THIS) you've eaten a piece of cake.

And the odds are extremely high that some of these cakes were from Betty Crocker. Now I'm sure many things come to mind when you think of her. Birthday cakes, your mom, and licking the bowl are probably a few.

But I bet you didn't know she was one of the most famous women and marketers in the 20th century. Her sales made Martha Stewart look like a mini-marshmallow.

And I also bet you didn't know Betty Crocker was….

A MAN!

WHAT DID BETTY CROCKER KNOW ABOUT SELLING THAT YOU DON'T?

Pay attention — you're going to learn MORE about one of the **strongest recipes** to make sure your idea will be a success.

However, let's dive into Betty's background first.

Here's a sales resource you've probably never checked out: "Finding Betty Crocker: The Secret Life of America's First Lady of Food" by Susan Marks

According to an interview done with Marks by CBS News This Morning…Back in the 1920's, "The Washburn Crosby Company ran an ad in the back of the Saturday Evening Post for their gold medal flour. And it was a puzzle, like a picture puzzle that you put together."

If you solved the puzzle, you won a pin cushion shaped like a sack of gold medal flour.

"It was an intoxicating lure," Marks points out, "because 30,000 people sent puzzles back expecting to get this little pin cushion. But what surprised the company was the couple hundred letters that also arrived asking for cooking and baking advice."

CREATE YOUR COMMUNITY OF RAVING FANS

Sam Gale, the company advertising director, decided to answer those letters. He even sent along recipes from the company's home economists. But when it came time to sign the letters, "He felt sort of strange about it," Marks says. "He thought a woman at home does not want advice from a man who supposedly doesn't know his way around the kitchen. …So he came up with the idea of Betty Crocker, a woman, who would answer this mail and be a friend to the homemaker."

Betty was invented by a man and then was represented by dozens of different people over the years.

"In fact in the height of Betty Crocker's popularity," Marks adds, "she got anywhere between 4,000 and 5,000 letters per day. The only known amount of mail that's more than that would be the amount that the Roosevelts got during the war. And that was about 7,000 a day."

And remember – this was in the 1920's.

So what did Betty know that you don't? (but you do NOW!)

You have to create a community of customers / prospects vs being someone who just SELLS STUFF to people.

BETTY KNEW ALL ABOUT PSY-CHOGRAPHICS EVEN IN THE 1920S!

- She wasn't stuffy and boring (even though her "parents" were General Mills)
- She didn't talk down to her customers.
- She knew her customers were too busy to make everything homemade BUT they wanted to FEEL they had a part in the cake. (Eliminated guilt)
- Her letters weren't written in the Third Person — but instead in a conversational and helpful tone.
- She wasn't a "one-hit wonder"

ARE YOU JUST SELLING STUFF? (OR THINKING ABOUT IT?)

C'mon. Be honest.

If you're just selling your product or service then you're not having your cake and eating it too. (Which IS POSSIBLE by the way!)

Do you ever wonder why sometimes customers buy from you and sometimes they don't?

What's missing?

The community of people who are your loyal, raving fans and who willingly refer you to others without even being asked. With each communication and connection they become the enthusiastic, unpaid sales force of what you do and how you do it.

The community will buy from you because you offer MORE than just info about your products/services and how to use them. You help your community solve their problems on a bigger level….one that they connect with emotionally.

And no whining! Don't get your apron in a knot. (Ha) You don't have to become Betty Crocker but you certainly can create a following like "she" had.

BETTY CROCKER HAD A RADIO SHOW – DO YOU EVEN HAVE A BLOG?

"In 1945, Fortune magazine named Betty Crocker the second most popular woman in America, behind that other first lady, Eleanor Roosevelt.

And, when the Betty Crocker big red picture cookbook first came out in 1950, sales rivaled those of the other big book, the Bible." reported by CBS TV.

It was the radio show that took Betty Crocker to superstardom. And this was over 50 years ago!

So let's say you're an accountant. And you have many entrepreneurs as clients. Well guess what? Entrepreneurs are interested in ANYTHING that helps them become better in business.

What could you do to help them RISE?

- Offer free lunch and learn sessions with experts
- Helpful posts on Twitter/Facebook and the newest and best of social media
- Blog cool tips
- Send out a bi-weekly e-zine (electronic newsletter)
- Mail out a printed newsletter
- Provide tips from sales and marketing experts, branding experts etc to help your customers navigate their sales
- Provide web site links, associations, resources and books

- Hold your own monthly webinars/video clips/ tele-classes (free for your customers) that you record and then send to them on CD or via an MP3 link.
- Create a mastermind group for your customers where they can meet for breakfast once per month and brainstorm.
- Podcasts/BlogTalk Radio show
- Twitter/Facebook and the newest and best of social media
- Postcards loaded with tips
- The list is endless!

You would move from being a "Bean Counter" to someone who is considered a valuable and positive resource.

I don't care what size of company you own or work for. With Facebook, Twitter, Linked In and Pinterest and so many other FREE TOOLS available you don't have an excuse. You can also create your own blog for free at www. wordpress.com or www.typepad.com. And you can ask to send your customers the latest tips and trends, interviews and ideas to help them create new opportunities.

You Want More Sales? Whip Up A Community!

Hmmm — maybe you're thinking *"Awww Sales Diva– this looks like work."*

Snap out of it.

Do you want to know what takes MORE WORK? Doing exactly what your competitors do, day after day, and being worried endlessly about your projections and repeat business. (ie/ sleepless nights and panicking about cash flow definitely apply here)

Because really. Taking your customers out for lunch or a round of golf once in a blue moon or sending them a random Christmas card and a fruit basket really isn't going to land you in their Hall of Fame.

I had a particularly resistant woman recently brag to me about how she has a wonderful yearly marketing strategy. She thought newsletters, ezines, social media and keeping in touch with her customers were over-rated activities. Instead…are you ready?

She sends out a calendar every year- the same boring magnetic calendar every sales rep in her organization across Canada sends out each Christmas.

The same calendar almost every lawyer, life-insurance agent, real-estate agent, car dealer, accountant, bank, local plumber, construction company, dentist, doctor or funeral home buys in mass from a huge national calendar company and inserts "their personal picture and contact information."

Wow. I'm dazzled.

With a Cheshire cat grin she said *"EVERYONE puts them on the fridge."*

Oh really? Well — aside from her grandmother **I don't think so**...not in today's world of choosing the calendar and message YOU want. (As IF I want a calendar with someone's branding all over it on my fridge. The only faces I want on my fridge are my guy, friends, family, and my dog!)

And the other point she completely missed?

Every other boring industry in the world does EXACTLY THE SAME THING and that is NOT how you build a community of customers.

Also it isn't something you can track the effectiveness of. You don't know who used it. You don't know who threw it out. You don't even know who received it. You can't track who opened it, who threw it away, who clicked on the link and bought from it, on what day, at what time... get my drift?

You also are sending it out ONCE PER YEAR which is barely enough contact to keep your old Aunt Martha happy.

REMEMBER – YOU CREATE A COMMUNITY WHEN IT IS ALL ABOUT THEM.

Regularly. It may be daily, weekly or monthly. The amount of contact is based on how often your customers want to hear from you and if they VALUE what you have to say.

The '50s are so over. And so are cheesy calendars and old school, out-dated forms of marketing.

(Are you listening to me life insurance/banking/real estate/car industries? Wake upppppppppppppppppp!)

My Diva-Dare For You?

Challenge yourself to connect with your past, current and future customers in unique and exciting ways.

Survey your customers. Ask them what would WOW them – find out what they're dying to know and do. Communicate with them regularly with info they wait anxiously for. Create a community of raving fans.

These people will help you turn your idea into something brilliant.

It's time to think outside of the cake box, cupcake!

CHAPTER ELEVEN:

Her Cakes Have Her Seeing Stars!

Anyone who knows me – understands I'm an addicted "magazine page ripper-outer." And they love me anyway! I have piles of ripped magazine pages – some organized – some not…but they all have caught my eye for one reason or another. I'm a complete research junkie.

Eventually they get sorted into folders – everything from gourmet cooking to when the average citizen can expect to fly to the moon (one of my lifetime goals).

Years ago an article in a national Canadian magazine caught my eye. The story was written about a Winnipeg, Manitoba (that's in Canada by the way) company that was selling delicious gourmet cakes…in hatboxes…and shipping them with fresh flowers and jewelry… around the world!

I thought it was a lovely and very cool idea (not to mention the fact I LOVE cake – anything lemon or chocolate - bring it on!)

So it went into the file labeled: "Interesting people I want to interview."

Fast forward a few years later. I went through the file again (now several inches thick!) and I sent Heather Stewart, the CEO of Lilyfield Cakes, a saucy request to be in my book.

She sent me back an equally saucy Yes.

Get ready for a really sweet entrepreneurial story!

Heather Stewart

CEO and Founder of Lilyfield Cakes www.lilyfieldcakes.com

Kim:	OK Lady - so what year did you start Lilyfield Cakes? Were visions of sugar plums dancing in your head?
Heather:	We started planning the business in 2000 and it came to fruition in 2001. (No sugar plums!) It took a while, the recipe took a while to sort out and then the box was the thing after that to make it so the cake fit in perfectly and make it so it could actually be shipped and not arrive broken.
Kim:	Exactly so it actually arrives looking like a cake vs a mashed pudding. So before we even talk about your cake company can I just get you to step

back in time? Were you a baker by heart with your Easy Bake oven?

Heather: I don't really even honestly know why I thought I could do this. I just thought I could so I thought "Why not try?"

Kim: **So what were you doing before you started? I know you're a proud mom.**

Heather: I was at home with my kids for 10 years. I hadn't worked in 10 years and honestly the reason the idea for Lilyfield Cakes started was because I needed to have some creative aspect to my life that really needed to be fulfilled. So before I started my business, I would go over the top with having parties and decorating and that sort of thing. I had a party once where I actually cut all the potatoes into the shape of stars.

I really needed an outlet! I had a Halloween party for my kids when my daughter was 3 and I actually cut this giant piece of white fabric, this roll of fabric, I cut ghosts that went behind all the pictures on the wall and all the mirrors. It was ridiculous!

Kim: **With the many women entrepreneurs I've coached over the years- their biggest stumbling block is they've really stopped and stifled themselves from moving forward with an idea.**

Heather: Fear of rejection.

Kim: **So Heather, … you were drinking a martini one night and you just decided "Hey I'm going to bake cakes and stick them in hat boxes and ship them internationally with all sorts of goodies inside." How did this happen?**

Heather: The woman who was my biz partner- we both really enjoyed entertaining. We wanted to find a way to take the idea a "party in a box" because it's good food and great presentation of a gift and fresh flowers. So that's where it came from because actually doing event planning where I live wasn't really feasible.

Also we knew at the beginning we wanted our business to be online because we could then pull from the whole world.

Heather: Lilyfield isn't even a hamlet- just has my farm and a church but I always loved the name. Long before I ever decided to have a business, I liked the name Lilyfield, I thought it sounded like such a magical place.

Kim: **So your business partner and you were together for what just a few years, 2 or 3 years?**

Heather: We started this together but our lives took different paths. I wanted the business to go really big and she had worked a long time, her kids were older, you know what I mean? This really wasn't what she envisioned.

Kim: **I went through something similar so I totally get you. It doesn't have to be the nasty break up or anything like that, it's just you come to fork in the road and you decide to part ways.**

So what kind of feedback did you get from the people around you when you said, *"Hey guys guess what, I think I'm going to launch a cake company?"*

Heather: Some people thought it was just stupid but it didn't matter. The people who did think that, I knew already. Most men thought it was stupid. I knew they didn't get it so it didn't bother me at all. I also was confident enough in my ability to create something really special and beautiful that I knew I would be all right. I knew that what I would make … people would like it.

And when I think of the first packages I made they weren't that great. They weren't at all what they are now!

Kim: **But you have to start somewhere.**

Heather: You do and then they just keep getting better. So then I knew there were some people who thought *"Yeah right, a cake in a box who cares?"* But as it turned out when people received them — they were thrilled!

Heather: Yes – people get so excited and sur-
            prised when they receive a Lilyfield
            Cake. So that's been great.

Kim: **Because every part of it is part of the
            experience, the cake box, the flowers
            (which I'm going to get into here in
            a second.) So some people supported
            you, some people thought you were
            nuts so…**

Heather: I think most people thought I was nuts.
            I'd say most people thought *"Yeah, good
            for you, good luck with that."* And I don't
            think anyone really thought it would
            succeed and I don't know why but I
            just confidently kept going.

Kim: **We all know when you start your
            business everything isn't smooth sail-
            ing. And actually what people want to
            learn about is that there were lumps
            and bumps. So what kind of lumps
            and bumps were in your "batter"?**

Heather: First of all getting the box figured out for
            the cake to fit in was a huge challenge.

Heather: It was complicated because the boxes are all hand-made and we had to figure out how we needed to make them and what material had to be used. And I had a lot of help from people. This one woman in particular, Sarah Mueller, she worked for a company called Advanced Paper Box at the time. She just knew exactly what to do.

There was another woman named Tara McTavish and she told us where to get wholesale fabric from Montreal. So just along the way people are willing to give you a hand and help you and you pay attention and listen to someone when they know something you don't.

Then it just went from there. So that was really hard and there definitely have been a few bumps. I have to do an FDA for every single package that goes into the US. So when that rule was first implemented it was like "Oh good Lord."

Kim: **Plus you also have to have a timely package. Your cake can't sit in customs** for 3 months. So who is making the cake?

Heather: I have a commercial baker here who bakes the cakes. Then I have people who make the boxes. So I make the first one and then they kind of follow them. So everything is sourced out and then it all comes together. Then we ship them off every day with Fed-Ex, they go overnight.

Kim: **So it's perfect timing for somebody to have cake and champagne the next day after they've had a celebration. You don't even require celebration; you just want to have a piece of cake!**

Heather: Well it could be for any occasion. That's the beautiful thing about this business is I get to send really good wishes between people. So even if it's a sad occasion, which sometimes it is, but most often its happy, it's still really nice to be in the middle of that.

Kim: **Heather-when did you decide to add some of the other components?**

Heather: From the beginning yes - it was cake first, flowers and then the little silver charm. The charm idea came from a Victorian custom of including cake charms and whatever the charm was that you got in your slice of cake was kind of your destiny.

So that was an original idea of the cake charms but, of course, I couldn't actually stick the charm in the cake. I didn't want someone to break their tooth on it! So it was just like an extra little thing and people seem to really like it. So that originally was all part of the first packages.

But I've really learned as I'm going along that you have to do something new all the time because it gets stale and boring.

Kim: **It does and people get used to it.**

Heather: Yes and to keep marketing your business you always need to have something fresh.

Kim: Let's talk about marketing. So when you first started, did you have some huge budget? Were you buying lots of advertising?

Heather: I've never bought advertising!

Kim: So what did you do? Here you were, in the tiny hamlet of Lilyfield and you have a web store and you. How did you decide "We're going to get on the web in a big way"… how did people find out about you? What did you do?

Heather: That's actually important because it's like you're online but if no one knows you're there you're not going to sell anything!

So you always have to be directing people there. I've always been a magazine freak. Sometimes I would buy them all and then I would have to wait for the next month to get something that interested me again. So I always had tons of magazines and I already understood they needed editorial content.

So the first summer before we launched I sent packages to Flare Magazine, to all the Canadian big magazines and I think we were in most of the Canadian magazines the first year.

Kim: So they had an opportunity to sample you in a physical way?

Heather: Yes and they're always looking for stuff.

Kim: They are absolutely. I come from the world of media but most people are intimidated by it.

Heather: I've just thought *"why wouldn't you like it?"*

Kim: Many women in biz think, *"what do I have that people can talk about me? Why me?"* Or they just get intimidated by someone they see as an anchor on TV or *"Wow- it's in one of the top magazines."* But you're actually doing these media a favor; they're always looking for editorial.

Heather: You're right; you're doing the media a favor. They are constantly looking for story ideas.

Kim: **So when you launched, you knew right away knew you needed to send news releases off to all the media and you sent off sample products. What else did you do?**

Heather: That's ALL I did.   I was in Lucky Magazine — that's what really put the business on the map and made it really viable.

Kim: **I love it!! So then it just moved viral and really went into word of mouth promotion.**

Heather: It did and I still find print is the best, being in an editorial part of a magazine is still the best way to promote my business because people trust editorials more then they trust advertising. They know that you're paying for the ad but they know if an editor or a columnist decides to include you in something it's because they like what you do.

But at the same time I also had a call from In Style magazine and I was supposed to be in their February issue as well and it didn't happen. At the time I was disappointed but I couldn't have handled it. It was just right to be in the first magazine and then you coast for a while and get another and keep going. Now, since most of the editors seem to know about my company, now they're interested when I have something as its easier for them. I really learned that because I've made some friends who helped me with PR and I've learned from their perspective what people are looking for. If they know you have a product that has a great reputation and it's really good, they're grateful to see what you have.

Kim: **Absolutely because all these magazines and media they're looking for the next best freshest thing as well.**

Heather: Yes it's true. I mean they don't always do something with what I have but I've been pretty lucky overall. I've had a great response and I continue to get good coverage and that's how I marketed my product. And I continue to do that.

Kim: **Do you have a strategy behind that Heather? Are you doing news releases every month? Are you sending out product every month? How often would you do that?**

Heather: I usually do it when I feel the need, which is kind of weird. It's like an ebb and flow thing and I feel the vibe.

Heather: I'll do a mailer and send product out to "x" amount of people. They know that its coming and then hopefully things are written and luckily that has kind of gone on.

And whenever there's an awards show or something "Hollywood-ish" there's always an opportunity if you're on a list of companies they like. And I get invited to a lot of those sorts of things and if I go to one it also helps to build my business.

Kim: **From what I understand you've been in some pretty significant events recently. You were at the Grammys weren't you?**

Heather: I was at the Grammy Gala which is the event they do as a fund raiser every year. They can eat as much cake as they want but basically I give them a certificate for a cake. And I only give the certificates to certain people who I can help and they can help me.

So I don't do any kind of mass certificates. But at the Grammys of course I gave certificates to celebrities like Tom Jones.

They are people who are essentially good. So you meet celebrities and they're just people - the same as you and I.

Kim: So you've also had celebrities like Halle Berry buy from you?

Heather: Yes she orders quite often.   S h e ' s been terrific and I've got a list of celebrities and I'm always really careful that I don't ever put them on my website or anything because I like to leave it at that level of…I don't want to be riding, liking hooking my chain on anyone else's star. If they're okay with it but I just think its better not to do that. I think being discreet just keeps my business at a certain level that I think they appreciate.

Kim: Absolutely. They don't feel they're being manipulated and yet on the other hand, when you're in business it definitely gives you an edge when people know you're attracting that type of clientele.

Heather: Its true and in this day and age when you want to be in some magazine they want to know what movie stars have bought your cake.

I will always ask for permission. So Halle Berry graciously said okay as did Virginia Madsen and Martina Mc-Bride and many more.

Kim: **What's so good about Lilyfield Cakes is that I think there's so much hope behind your entire story.**

Heather: I agree with you and I love it that you see it that way too. For goodness sake, I live in the middle of Canada in a really small place but the world is really open to you if you're open to it.

Kim: **People think they have to be super connected and have this massive advertising budget. They have to do all this stuff to actually have a thriving business when NO... you just have to have a back bone versus a wish bone.**

Kim: **Everyone has made a cake that's flopped. So tell me about a flop.**

Heather: I stuck with a baker a little too long then I should have before I let him go but it's worked out. And UPS has gone to hell in a hand basket and I stuck with them longer then I should have too.

Kim: **There's the perception that switching to something different is going to take a massive amount of work.**

Heather: It does take some work and you're right- that was why I held off. I'm also one of those people that I don't ever want to upset anybody or hurt anyone's feelings. I always think they're going to do better, they mean well and sometimes we just have to let it go.

So the people I end up working with I don't often ever have a problem. I'll have to tell you though I did have one situation where I hired someone to do some PR and because of where I am she represented a champagne company and kind of sold me on the fact that she understood fine food. I thought "All right this is going to be a good fit. She seems to know what she's talking about" and it was awful. Luckily it didn't last very long. A couple of red flags came up almost immediately and after 3 months I let her go.

But what I've noticed though is something good always comes of it. Every event I've done or everyone that I've met — there's always something good that comes out of it. And through that disaster she actually introduced me to the woman who does PR with me now who lives in Los Angeles.

Kim: **Give your words of wisdom to a woman entrepreneur today. She's hanging in there but she's starting to lose the steam even though she knows she has a good product. But the bills are starting to get her down, what advice would you recommend to her?**

Heather: Two things, establish a really good relationship with your banker, a personal relationship so you can get to know them and they really know who you are and what you're capable of doing and what you're going to do. And the other thing is just don't quit. Everybody says that but it's really true.

Kim: **What did Eleanor Roosevelt say, "When you're at the end of your rope tie a knot in it and hang on?"**

Heather: You just don't quit. Last year was a starting off point all over again. I can feel the momentum and I'm really excited to have new ideas and bring them to market.

Kim: **So how do you brainstorm all your new ideas? You've got all these things happening and again when someone is reading this they're going "Okay I've got my one idea" and you keep saying "Yes, but you've got to come up with the next idea." So what do you find fuels you? What do you find inspires those new, the patty cake idea? Where does that come from?**

Heather: I think always paying attention.

Kim: You're in the love mail business because when you go to your mailbox or when you have somebody come to the door its like "Oh God, what bill is coming to me or what is happening?" and then you get this fabulous woo-hoo cake box, it doesn't get any better than that!

Heather: I know it's very fun and I often hear from people who write me nice notes and say what the reaction was from the person they sent it to and it makes you feel wonderful.

Kim: It does. It's not just a cake. You're creating an experience, which of course when you create an experience you create a memory.

I remember reading years ago that the nicest gift you can ever give someone is a memory.

And that's what YOU do Heather.

Heather: Thank you!

Well as you've probably guessed – 2 days after this inter-view, I came home from a meeting and there…waiting on my doorstep was this big brown box from Lilyfield Cakes! Honestly – I jumped up and down in my stilettos!

What a treat!

Even opening it was an experience. Beautiful tissue, gor-geous ribbon, a vintage style hat-pin that held the fresh flower bouquet together, a silver charm bracelet in a box, more gorgeous tissue and then…the piece de resistance… this fantastic dark chocolate cake. You know the really heavy, moist kind that calls to you passionately at 2 am in the morning?

Heavy sigh…I'm wishing I had a piece of it right now!!

All I can say is…I had cake crumbs in my lipstick for a few days. Cake is a marvelous food group…especially for breakfast. (And especially one from Lilyfield Cakes!)

CHAPTER TWELVE:

Why Do Ideas Fly or Flop?

Sizzled or fizzled.
Frazzled or flunked.
Flew or flopped.
Towered or toppled.
Sailed or sunk.

(Hmmm – I could have been Dr. Seuss.)

You've seen a few thousand ideas like these in your time. They came – they went. Yawn. Dig deeeep into your memory bank, lady.

WHAT IDEAS HAVE BEEN HUNG OUT TO DRY?

Pet rocks
The Yellow Pages
Platform boots
8-track cassette tapes
Acid wash jeans

Tiffany
The McRib.
Vanilla Ice
The New Coke
Cabbage Patch dolls
Furby
VCRs
Charlie perfume
MC Hammer pants
Blockbuster

WHAT HAS HUNG IN THERE?

Lego
U2
Big Mac
The New York Times
Jane Eyre
Tiffanys
Barbie
7-11
Oprah
Chanel
Nike
Harley Davidson
Madonna
Levis Jeans
TIDE

So what's the difference between "what's hung in there" vs what's been "hung out to dry?"

The **long-lasting ideas** have the ability to hit a deep emotional chord, flexibility, creativity, willingness to change with the times while still offering exceptional value and meeting and exceeding the needs of its consumer. They live in the land of REINVENTION.

The **ideas that disappeared** quickly were usually based on a fad, short-term technology, fashion, resisted changing with the times, didn't meet and exceed the needs of their customers and didn't develop relationships with new waves of consumers. That's not a checkmate – it's a stalemate.

So do you plan on disappearing or sticking around?

One of my favorite authors, Seth Godin (he's my secret brain crush) wrote this on his blog www.sethgodin.com:

"If you want to grow, you need new customers. And if you want new customers, you need three things:

1. A group of possible customers you can identify and reach.
2. A group with a problem they want to solve using your solution.
3. A group with the desire and ability to spend money to solve that problem.

You'd be amazed at how often new businesses or new ventures have none of these. The first one is critical, because if you don't have permission, or knowledge, or word of mouth, you're invisible."

As Seth mentions — you need an audience you can reach, an audience with a problem they're willing to pay YOU money to fix and **they gotta have the desire and money, honey.**

Here's another mistake I see.

THE MISTAKE OF RIDING INTO THE SUNSET

One of the biggest mistakes made is to launch an idea and then think you'll never have to tweak it. You dust your hands and say *"There Ma — I did it!"*

And then you ride your pony into the sunset.

Ummm. That's not a strategy.

You have to become the:

Queen of Tweakers.
Madame of Reinvention
Empress of Reinvention.

Now don't get your nylons in a knot.

WHY DO IDEAS FLY OR FLOP?

You CAN do this.

Because if you're willing to grow out AND up (remember my redwood tree story!) you'll discover new opportunities, new customer niches, new ways of attracting attention and new ways of making money. Don't worry about going through *Ugly-Baby-itis* again. It's never ending!

So Which One Is Your Mantra?

1. **If It Ain't Broke Don't Fix It?**

2. **Back To The Drawing Board!**

The "If It Ain't Broke Don't Fix It" mantra is the **kiss of death** for your idea.

Why?

Ideas, products, services should feel "alive and fresh" not old and stuffy.

Guess what?

The earth isn't flat, butter doesn't heal a burn, eggs are good for you, your face won't stick like that, and an old dog can learn new tricks. (Especially my little black dog – she's brilliant.)

If I were you, I'd embrace **"Back to the drawing board."**

It doesn't mean you have to stall your plans, pull up stakes and not forge ahead. It means your idea should ALWAYS be on the drawing board, being improved, adjusted, realigned and reinvented. Plus — it's a lot more fun and will stop you from experiencing this…..

THE SIGNS OF IDEA RIGOR MORTIS

Remember some of the out-right flops and short-term fads I mentioned at the beginning of this chapter? Well — what they all have in common is RIGOR MORTIS.

Yup. Stiff as a board. No flexibility. Couldn't or wouldn't change. And have you ever heard of this quote?

> *"The only difference between a grave
> and a rut are the dimensions."*

Make sure you watch out for these signs of Idea Rigor Mortis…and be careful — they can sneak up on you while you're "procrastinating and perfecting!"

OBSESSION – MORE THAN A PERFUME

I mentioned in an earlier chapter about being too close to your idea. You're so in love with it that you aren't willing to see the fault lines. You won't even acknowledge there are any flaws in fact. And of course, this is a HUGE FLAW in itself, lady.

Some people not as nice as I am would even say you're OBSESSED. It's happened to all of us. This little book came damn close to being an obsession because I was soooooo excited by it. (One of the first signs you're losing your marbles)

You're obsessed with perfecting "your baby".

Quit waiting for pigs to fly, stars to align, ducks to get in a row and for your lucky skirt to come back from the dry-cleaner. There's someone who can help you with your idea RIGHT NOW except you've forgotten completely about them. Or you need to ask someone to hook you up with someone who knows someone. Ha.

In fact, I bet as soon as you read the paragraph above SOMEONE just popped into your head. Connect with them asap! That's an order!

WHO IS THE BEST PERSON FOR YOUR IDEA??

I know what you THOUGHT I was going to say.

You thought I was going to say YOU. (TOLD you I have ESP)

Well – yes I acknowledge your very important role in the creation of an idea.

However – there's a *forgotten about person* who actually has **far more say, influence and control** over the sustainability of your idea. They are the general in the background calling all the shots – so you'd better take a good look at them and listen well.

The forgotten about person?

YOUR CUSTOMER.

Do You Know What Pushes The Hot Buttons On Your Customer?

Remember – your product or service has to fulfill a DEEP DESIRE in your customer. It has to have something that motivates them and moves them to action on both a conscious and subconscious level.

Example: Dog food.

This is a pretty boring product. It's about as much fun as buying toilet paper. There are 12 million brands, they all have the happy dog on the front and they all say "It's healthy" for your dog. And many of us sometimes "cheap out" and buy the supermarket premium dog food because we think it will do the job.

My little black dog is 13 years old, she's an absolute joy and she recently had her annual check-up. Overall, she's in great health but she was getting a little pudgy.

This very cool old vet – he calls himself "Dr. Al" checked her over and said "She's having a little trouble with her hips?"

I said *"Yes – she's definitely been slowing down these past 6 months."*

He looked at me, looked at my little black dog and said *"Well –it's a circle. She's got some arthritis and she then doesn't want to move as much – which makes her gain weight and then she doesn't want to move… which makes her gain weight."*

And he said the magic hot button words:

"If she DOESN'T lose some weight, she'll be in pain and will probably lose 2-3 years off her life span."

GASP!

Why DO YOU buy expensive diet dog food for your dog?

Because you love how your dog elevates your life.

The love, the fun, the cuddles, the Frisbee throwing moments – your dog is one of your best friends. And you want her to be happy, healthy and IN YOUR LIFE as long as possible.

So what do you do? You buy the expensive diet dog food from the vet so she can keep running, jumping and bounding up the stairs without pain. Quite frankly – it makes you feel better knowing she feels better.

I bought the expensive dog food, denied her all of her extra treats and she's also on this smelly stuff called Sasha's Blend. (This powdered seafood mixture from Australia helps their joints –it's awesome) and of course, her weight has come down, she's running up and down the stairs without pain and I'm thrilled!

All my logic and beliefs about premium dog food went out the window. Instead, what Dr. Al said hit me on a deep level – of how much I love my little black dog. Plus – he's credible, caring, trustworthy, AND he was right.

It also shows why this veterinarian who has a reputation of kindness and a sense of humor – has STAYED IN business for over 25 years. Everything he's doing is congruent with who he is. You can FEEL IT.

There are always 4 cats perched up by the debit machine – honestly, you have to swoosh their tail over to type in your pin number. (Cat security!) They have tons of pictures of all their happy patients – a huge mural is on the wall. It isn't a sterile and stuffy atmosphere.

P.S. How did I find out about Dr. Al and his fabulous service? Well my sister and my 2 cute nieces "Good Gossiped" about him. Dr. Al had them walk right into the back of the clinic and he explained everything to the kids about their puppy…and he cracked them up with his bad jokes. He's kind, big-hearted, has a deep love of animals and my little black dog looked at him with adoration.

Dr. Al is "spreadable" and he isn't an idea that has fizzled. Plus he has cats for secretaries. Pretty cool. (I think they can type 100 wpm.)

Discover Your Customer's Hot Buttons

If you DON'T KNOW the hot buttons of your hot market for your supposed HOT idea – then you're going to struggle.

It's just that simple. And here's the guy to help you.

It's Time To Interrupt This Program With A Commercial

Well – it's not technically a commercial but it is certainly about one of the super stars who MADE commercials.

One of the world's most famous ad men is Paul Arden. His book **"It's Not How Good You Are, It's How Good You Want To Be"** initially sounds like a self-help manual.

It's not.

In fact, you won't find any references to Mars or Venus here.

Paul's book "uses the creative processes of good advertising as a metaphor for business practices." I love it. It's a major kick in the ass actually.

Paul challenges the status quo and does it on purpose.

He knows there will be times his idea will be booted out of the building, cut down to size etc. HOWEVER, he also knows he stands a far greater chance of SUCCEED-ING by consistently putting good ideas out there.

In a successful advertising agency it is ALWAYS about the idea and the odds of a client turning it down are high.

As Paul says:

> *"Find out what the client's real objective is.*
> *All clients aspire to status."*

He also has this brilliant piece of advice I want you to roll around in your mind and savor like a good piece of chocolate:

> *"When it can't be done, do it. If you don't do it, it*
> *doesn't exist."*

You need to get your idea out of your head and computer and OUT THERE.

So there.

CHAPTER THIRTEEN:

Have You Fallen And Can't Get Up?

This is a short and not so sweet chapter on failure, struggle, feeling side-swiped and what to do when the chips are down and the shit has hit the fan.

Failure can feel like a bitter little cyanide pill can't it?

Back in the early '80s there was a campy commercial for a medical alarm and protection service for seniors.

The commercial sold a medical pendant with an audio device in it and the very bad actors would say…

"I've fallen and I can't get up!"

And the medical alarm service would answer their cry for help and send an ambulance.

When you're working on an idea and you're feeling beat-up by obstacles — whether they are financial or otherwise — you probably feel like yelling out…

"I've fallen and I can't get up!"

The problem is so many of us are reluctant to ask for help or to even admit we have a problem. Pride. Stubbornness. Guilt. Embarrassment. Anger. All of these emotions can hold us back from asking for what we need.

So we just end up "lying on the cold bathroom floor" and no one knows we even need help!

Every single woman I know in business has met hardship at some point. Problems related to finances, family, health, lack of support, staff (or even finding any), red tape, divorce, death, revenue agencies — eesh — it can feel pretty ugly and hopeless at times.

This is why I've interviewed someone who not only crashed but rose from the ashes, like the famous mythical bird the Phoenix, more glorious and alive than before.

Gail Hall is a very successful entrepreneur who runs a cooking school and culinary travel adventures around the world.

Gail and I met in a funky little coffee shop and she eagerly shared her story, the ups, the downs with a transparency I only see (and recognize) in people who've been to the bottom and bounced back up. Why? The downward spiral scraped them clean and allowed them to bounce back lighter.

Gail came from an entrepreneur family – her dad had several successful businesses in the food industry in Toronto, (he even owned a pickle factory) but due to events beyond his control, he went bankrupt.

"My dad had so much gumption – he never gave up. Even when he went bankrupt he found another way to make a living for his family."

Gail takes a thoughtful sip of her coffee, leans in toward me and says…

"But it left me with a secret fear of going bankrupt."

As an avid foodie, in 1985 Gail eventually decided to open up a catering business in Edmonton, Alberta, Canada called Gourmet Goodies.

Over the next 10 years she owned a 4200 square foot building, had 45 staff, and $110,000 payroll per month.

"I was severely in the red. I never slept as I was worrying about clients and staff, how to improve the food, the business – you name it."

Just as they were preparing for a busy and prosperous Christmas season - September 11, 2001 happened. And all corporate business came to a grinding halt. The Christmas season, which is "the big Kahoona" for caterers, didn't happen. All corporate events dried up and people were staying at home.

By January 2002 she was even deeper in the red but continued to struggle and focus on keeping her head above water.

Gail sighs.

"My bank wouldn't return any of my phone calls. I was panicking. I cashed in all of my RRSPs. When the bank did finally meet with me – in early 2003, they gave me 60 days to come up with the money for both my line of credit and my mortgage on the building."

By July 2003 she had to close her company and walk away from a building that was worth over 1 million dollars and was almost paid off.

She said *"My husband John has always believed in me and he lost the money too. But we decided we were not going to let this destroy us."*

For the next 2 years Gail worked in retail and in customer service. But entrepreneurship was still in her blood.

"In 2005 I started cooking classes in our condo. So far I've taught over 2,000 people with my company Seasoned Solutions. Then John told me I should build travel into my business. We've now taken clients on 16 culinary adventures – Italy, France, New Zealand, New York and so many other lovely places. My clients want to travel and appreciate

the food in different cultures and then they want to come home and recreate the food here with local ingredients."

Gail laughs delightedly, *"This business has exceeded all of our expectations!"*

But building new businesses wasn't her only obstacle. In June 2008 she was dealt a blow of a different sort. Breast cancer.

"I had a culinary tour in 3 weeks with 25 people. I came home and had surgery, 6 rounds of chemo, 25 rounds of radiation and I worked through-out it all. It was my highest year ever and I also know it kept me focused on living."

Since then, Gail has been a radio columnist and continues with her uber- successful cooking school and culinary travel adventures. Her passion for what she's doing is contagious!

"I have no regrets. There's so much MORE I want to do with food!"

Gail's List of Advice For Entrepreneurs:

1. Do the research.
2. Your product/service HAS to be different and serve a niche.
3. It doesn't have to be about price.

4. Test it. Ie/ volunteer for a B & B if that is your dream.
5. Ask for help.
6. Don't keep your line of credit and business mortgage at the same bank. You're trapped.
7. Cut your costs.
8. Be willing to be flexible. Sometimes you need to change your formula.
9. Accept criticism.
10. You need to react FAST if there's a problem.
11. Make decisions on logic and not emotion.
12. You have to learn how to say no.

SHE HAD THE NOT-SO-SMALL-POTATO JOURNEY

Angela Santiago is CEO and co-owner of The Little Potato Company. Her company grows those cute, creamy and delicious little potatoes we all love.

And her family-owned business certainly isn't "small potatoes" in North America.

Angela and her father had a dream to grow and sell "baby potatoes" to food distributors and grocery chains around the world. Except they didn't own a farm, had never studied agriculture or even been raised on a farm.

Oh. And Angela was a green as grass 20 something year old and her dad was in the drywall taping business.

To grow and sell baby potatoes was an idea her dad came up with after he was chatting with some Dutch farmers. As a Dutch immigrant, he longed for the creamer potatoes of his youth that he couldn't find in Canada.

After he spoke with his daughter about it – they decided to jump in – planting the potatoes by hand, washing them in bathtubs, marketing and selling them at local farmers markets. Soon, the demand was high and restaurant chefs started calling. Angela juggled everything for 3-5 years and then got married, had kids and the company stayed the same size for several years.

And then they decided they didn't want to be a "small potato" company in terms of size any longer.

They found national and international distributors for the product. They grew to a multi-million dollar business, expanded the staff and yet they made sure they stayed with the strong values that had made them successful in the first place.

BUT HILLS AND VALLEYS HAPPEN TO EVERY BUSINESS

Angela says, *"I was working 100 miles a minute. I had high stress, was worrying all the time, not getting enough sleep. And of course, I was trying to focus time and energy on my family too as I'm a passion-ate mom.*

It wasn't sustainable.

When I was 39 I was diagnosed with breast cancer. I beat it, changed my habits and with the support of my family, friends and my employees – the company kept moving forward and so did I. My life is very rich!"

The goal Angela has for her company? *"To sell 1 lb of potatoes, per person, per year, in every country in the world."*

Some Angela Advice For You?

1. You're more capable than you give yourself credit for.
2. Stay in motion. The answers will come. But if you stand still the answers will NOT come.

Hey listen. Feeling like a failure sucks. It really does.

If you've experienced the BOMB and you're feeling like you want to stay in your pajamas for the rest of your life and hide from the world – I want to give your bed a shake.

You're not a failure. Not at all, Ms. Pajamas. You're a risk taker, a dreamer, a "do-er", and you've done something most people won't even try to do.

Sure. Maybe you could have done things differently. But you can't magically go back into the past and revise those decisions. All you can do is face what is real, accept responsibility, learn from it and also take all the goodness from the experience.

This may be the DETOUR you needed to take in order to achieve an even larger or more joyful goal. And although right now it feels like a pain in the ass (and probably in your heart too) I'd bet you're on your way to something marvelous.

And so as the old song goes....

"Pick yourself up, dust yourself off, and start all over again."

CHAPTER FOURTEEN

It's Time For Action

I really appreciate you've made it this far!

It means you're serious.

It's Time For Action, Lady.

However, I don't want you to fall into the TRAP so many women fall into.

It's when you confuse ACTION with ACTIVITY.

I love reading philosophy. One of my favorite philosophers is Osho (although he would never have called himself a philosopher)

He wrote a lovely book called **Creativity: Unleashing the Forces Within** and this passage changed my life:

"Action is when the situation demands it and you act, you respond. Activity is when the situation doesn't matter, it is not a response; you are so restless within that situation it is just an excuse to be active.

Action is when it has relevance; activity is irrelevant."

You're heard or said these phrases before:

- I'm SO busy
- I feel like I'm spinning my wheels
- I'm working like a mad woman
- It feels like a circus
- Too much to do and not enough time to do it
- I need more than 24 hours a day
- I feel like I've worked all day and accomplished nothing
- All I do is race around from one thing to the next

Osho would think you've entered the zone of destruction.

"Action is creative. Activity is destructive —
it destroys you, it destroys others."

-Osho

It's time for you to create a PLAN OF ACTION vs winging it with activities that aren't relevant or important.

You're going to love this story.

A few years ago I read about a Canadian woman in her mid-40's who moved to Paris after she was there ONCE. As soon as she arrived back in Canada, she sold her PR firm, rented her apartment and moved to Paris to start an English speaking tour company for women.

I contacted Karen Henrich immediately as I was headed to Paris in 2 weeks and wanted her to be our personal guide.

She was a delight. Not only had she created a new life for herself in Paris (and did I mention she barely spoke a word of French when she moved there??), she had embraced the culture, the people, the clothes, the attitude and was showing the secrets of Paris to women all over the world with customized walking tours.

Karen and I sipped a glass of champagne at the champagne bar in Galeries Lafayette, the luxurious French department store and we gazed overhead at the historic and impressive stained glass ceiling.

I asked her where she found the courage to do something that so many people dream about but most will never do.

I'll never forget what she said.

"I couldn't NOT do it.
The desire to come to Paris was so strong;
I knew I had to follow
what my heart was telling me."

Now Karen is married, lives in both Vancouver and in Paris, owns www.chicwalks.com and has expanded her walking tours to many other international cities.

She's a girl who walks her talk!

THE LIFE OF A DAY
– TOM HENNEN

Like people or dogs, each day is unique and has its own personality quirks which can easily be seen if you look closely. But there are so few days as compared to people, not to mention dogs, that it would be surprising if a day were not a hundred times more interesting than most people. But usually they just pass, mostly unnoticed, unless they are wildly nice, like autumn ones full of maple trees and hazy sunlight, or if they are grimly awful ones in a winter blizzard that kills the lost traveler and bunches of cattle. For some reason we like to see days pass, even though most of us claim we don't want to reach our last one for a long time. We examine each day before us with barely a glance and say, no, this isn't one I've been looking for, and wait in a bored sort of way for the next, when, we are convinced, our lives will start for real. Meanwhile, this day is going by perfectly well adjusted, as some days are, with the right amounts of sunlight and shade, and a light breeze scented with a perfume made from the mixture of fallen apples, corn stubble, dry oak leaves, and the faint odor of last night's meandering skunk.

*What perfect day are you waiting for?

THE MAGICAL 15 MINUTES

Do you know you can do ANYTHING for 15 minutes a day?

I know one thing for sure, pumpkin.

YOU WILL REGRET LETTING YOUR IDEA DIE.

If you keep running around "being busy" … your precious dreams will wither and shrivel like vegetables in your fridge "Crisper Drawer" as they aren't being given the attention they deserve. (I call it the "Souper". Why? I'll give you 3 guesses.)

Remember – your idea doesn't get to stay with you forever.

At this very minute, someone else out in the world is start-ing to dream up something EXACTLY LIKE IT – or very close to it.

So dilly-dallying and thinking you can sit on this forever is ridiculous.

15 MINUTES PER DAY GREASES THE WHEELS

You could spend 15 minutes checking out your favorite social media site or watching TV or you could CHOOSE to give energy to something really important to you.

Only 15 minutes a day creates momentum – it ends up with a magical life of its own – it becomes effortless. (It's how I wrote this book – 15 minutes at a time!)

I'm reminding you again of the quote from grouchy speaker and internet guru called Dan Kennedy. Some-thing he said always motivates me whenever I catch myself in Dilly-Dally Mode.

"MONEY LOVES SPEED."

– Dan Kennedy

So yes, you do need a plan and all that jazz.

But you have to put it into ACTION so you can create the speed that attracts money!

MY BOSSY ADVICE?

Now that you've whipped through the chapters of this book ONCE —I want you to go back and re-read each chapter. I mean it, smartie-pants.

At the end of each chapter I want you to choose 3 BABY STEPS you can start TODAY.

Don't be afraid.

Right now…what you're so afraid of is a gift that only YOU can unwrap.

Your dream is waiting for you.

And it isn't UGLY. In fact, it may be the very thing…the very thing you will be MOST proud of for the rest of your life.

So there.

WHAT 6 IMPOSSIBLE THINGS BEFORE BREAKFAST WILL YOU DO?

"There is no use trying,"
said Alice; "one can't
believe impossible things."
"I dare say you haven't had
much practice," said the Queen.
"When I was your age, I always did
it for half an hour a day. Why,
sometimes I've believed as many
as six impossible things
before
breakfast."

–Lewis Carroll

Acknowledgements:

A special thank you, hugs and martinis to Jeanne Fitz-maurice, Karen Luniw, Heather Stewart, Gail Hall, Angela Santiago, Ernie Zelinski, Debbie Mrazek, Angela Armstrong, Jo-Ann Dibblee, Laurel Vespi, Tina Pratt, Susan Fitzsimmons, Sandra Hanna, Bev Norman and Johwanna Alleyne who all helped in their own fabulous and unique way to make this *"Ugly Baby"* come to life.

Also a big thank you to my thousands of subscribers, friends, fans and followers – I absolutely LOVE writing for you each week! Through you – I've discovered me.

And to R. Same.

Notes:

Chapter 2: The Bad Habit of Being Stuck

"Of speãal interest is Cathedral Grove, where delegates who drafted the charter of the United Nations held a commemorative ceremony on May 19, 1945, in tribute to President Franklin D. Roosevelt, who died in April of that year."

* Source: MSN Travel.com

Robert Frost, *The Road Not Taken* (*Mountain Interval,* Henry Holt and Company, 1916)

Chapter 3: Thinking About "What If"

Evelyn McFarlane and James Saywell, *The Big Book of If* (Random House, Inc. 2002)

Chapter 5: All Or Nothing Is For Sissies
Langston Hughes, *A Dream Deferred*, <u>The Collected Poems of Langston Hughes</u> by <u>Langston Hughes</u> and <u>Arnold Rampersad</u> (Vintage; 1st Vintage classics ed edition October 31, 1995)

*"Subway stores began appearing in **unusual locations**, <u>catering</u> to consumers where they might not expect a sandwich shop--at convenience stores and truck stops." Source: JustAskTheDoctor.com*

Chapter 6: The Art of Looking Sideways

Alan Fletcher, *The Art of Looking Sideways*, (Phaidon Press, August 20, 2001)

Chapter 7: Are You Calling My Baby Ugly?

Louis Simpson, *Ed;* Good Poems by Garrison Keillor (Penguin Books; 1ST edition August 26, 2003)

Mary Lou Quinlan, *Just Ask A Woman*, (Wiley; 1 edition, April 25, 2003)

Chapter 10: Create Your Community Of Raving Fans

Susan Marks, *Finding Betty Crocker: The Secret Life of America's First Lady of Food,* (Univ Of Minnesota Press; 1 edition, March 19, 2007)

Chapter 11: Why Do Ideas Fly Or Flop?

Paul Arden, *It's Not How Good You Are, It's How Good You Want To Be,* (Phaidon Press; 1st edition, June 1, 2003)

Chapter 14: It's Time For Action

Osho, *Creativity: Unleashing the Forces Within,* (St. Martin's Griffin; 1st edition (1999)

Tom Hennen, *The Life of a Day,* Good Poems by Garrison Keillor (Penguin Books; IST edition August 26, 2003)

Lewis Carrol, *Alice in Wonderland,* (Dover Publications (May 20, 1993)

53751576R00148

Made in the USA
Charleston, SC
19 March 2016